Dog People

WRITERS AND ARTISTS ON CANINE COMPANIONSHIP

Dog People

WRITERS AND ARTISTS ON CANINE COMPANIONSHIP

Edited by Michael J. Rosen

ILLUSTRATIONS BY

Amy and David Butler

ARTISAN · NEW YORK

For Mark, one good dog, and for the other two

Designer: Jim Wageman
Assistant designer: Jennifer S. Hong
Production director: Hope Koturo

Published in 1995 by Artisan,
a division of Workman Publishing Company, Inc.
708 Broadway New York, NY 10003

Library of Congress Cataloging-in-Publication Data
Dog People: writers and artists on canine
companionship/edited by Michael J. Rosen;
illustrations by Amy and David Butler.
ISBN 1-885183-17-8
    1. Dogs—United States—Anecdotes.
    2. Dogs—United States—Pictorial works.
    3. Authors, American—Anecdotes.
    4. Artists—United States—Anecdotes.
    5. Dog owners—United States—Anecdotes.
    6. Dogs—Social aspects—United States.
I. Rosen, Michael J., 1954–
SF426.5.D59 1995
818'.5403—dc20
[B]   95-23914

Printed in Hong Kong
10 9 8 7 6 5 4 3 2 1
First Printing

CONTENTS

LIVING IN A DOGMOCRACY

Send "a photo of your face and a photo of your dog's face," a recent advertisement in a dog fancier's magazine recommends. "See yourself as the real Dog Person you are," and through some pyrotechnic photo-imaging process, you'll receive a hybridized portrait that selectively breeds for the best human and canine features. The resulting photo will texture your smooth skin with fur, sculpt your hair into prick or bat or rose ears, extend the slope of your nose into a black-tipped muzzle . . . until that old cliché about a person coming to resemble his or her dog is proved with hard photographic evidence.

Somehow, I resist sending a check and the requisite snapshots, though I am unmistakably a "dog person," as is, I suspect, every contributor who donated work for this book. But I have different ideas about dog people, age-old ideas that hardly require a computer, or even a camera.

This sympathetic association is not a melding of two species' physical characteristics, but a metaphorical marriage: two different families—Canidae and Hominidae—

share a life together, appreciating as well as accommodating their differences. We've trained dogs to abide our limited notions of territory, forgo the hunt, sleep indoors (on or off the furniture), obey words that hardly resemble their mother tongue, and generally accept us as members of their pack—most often top dog. Dogs, well, it might be harder to recite exactly what dogs have trained us to do, though some working ideas follow, not only in my introduction, but throughout the pages of *Dog People*.

People and dogs have cohabited successfully for longer than anyone has been writing down statistics, such as that, on average, a human-human alliance—that "marriage" thing— lasts about seven years, or the loose equivalent of a single dog year. In light of the accelerating estrangements and separations rife within our society, our relations with dogs remain some of the longest-standing, mutually beneficial ones we humans have. That human-canine bond has lasted well over 12,000 years; all dog books are obliged to mention that number.

While dogs have, willingly or unwillingly, lent us upstanding apes their keen ears, extraordinary noses, big teeth, strong backs, four-footed speed, and tenacious will to track or dig or fight (to say nothing of their literal sacrifices for our wars and space travel and medical research), companionship has been the one perpetual, frequently equitable, arrangement. And people have only managed to accomplish this once in the five hundred millennia we've traipsed around worrying the rest of creation. Sure, we've subjugated a few blessed beasts with greater and lesser success (depends on which creature you interview); harvested quite a lot of them for the dinner table; tolerated the vast majority at a not-always-comfortable distance; confined a few within the miniature arenas called "our homes"; struck up a cordial détente with at least one other, the cat; and put an unfathomable number out of the nature business entirely.

Dog People presents original work by writers and artists who share two things beyond the distinction of their artistic accomplishments: the recognition that dogs have held a significant place in their lives, and the recognition that lots of other dogs aren't as lucky. Millions are abandoned, surrendered, and abused by non-dog people every year. Many dog people, meanwhile, make a vocation or avocation of dogs—training, showing, breeding, or caring. But contributors to this book (with a few exceptions) have simply made families that include dogs. Their extraordinary capacity to give voice to the powerful, undiluted feelings dogs engender within us is what makes each author and artist an exceptional dog person. I took pleasure, certainly, but also great comfort in reading each new essay, nodding in agreement, in recognition of my own experiences with dogs. We trust ourselves to interpret so much of our dogs' lives, and these articulate dog people affirm the responses and reasons we tentatively assign to what we suspect and hope the dog feels. They affirm the unaccountable intensity of our feelings toward our animals—something we often can't express. They'll also focus whatever lingering irritation you, too, may possess regarding the word "anthropomorphism," or that opposite, benighted piece of logic that says dogs, as instinctual machines, have no feelings.

If only our dogs could read these tributes! But then, it wouldn't alter their egos much. What well-kept dog doesn't already have its virtues extolled each day in obedience work, welcome-home rituals, walking or waking-up sessions? Dogs take their virtues for granted, never for a moment worrying about accomplishing this or atoning for that before the dreaded approach of death. But the foreknowledge of death leaves us reading creatures less confident.

Would dogs write such testimonies about us if they could? Would there be a companion volume, *People Dogs?* I'd wager not. Dogs' lives are already perfect—or at least they should be—and it's only imperfection that leads to writing. As the poet Richard Howard argues: "It's the fallen angel who is the recorder. In heaven, there's nothing for us to write about." Life on earth should be heaven for dogs. They train us to be a little more angelic, to see our virtues as well as the ones we lack.

Dog people are folks who want their lives to be a little doggier—more physical contact, consistency, innocence, wildness, routine, unselfconsciousness, and even humility. Observing a dog is an exercise in appreciating the gifts of the nonhuman. Dog people try to put more "nature" in the concept of human nature. Dog people feel that seeing their dog basking on a sunny pane of carpet is a good reason to snuggle up for a snooze; they take the thumping tail as reassurance that yielding to the moment was the right decision. They like being greeted each time they've been away, a reminder that life is too unbearably short to feign indifference to any joy, however familiar and constant. Dog people appreciate a dog's expectations: *Now is when we walk. Now is when I hop on the bed and you massage my ears. Now comes the part when you say you'll be right back but I know you won't be home before dinner.* Dog people's souls are anchored by the gravity of another creature's simpler needs.

So, enough about dog people. Let's get to dogs. My dogs.

Morning Walk. Shortly after waking, my retrievers begin an impatient ritual of stretches, vocalizations, unsolicited toy-bringing, play bows, and so on until my shoes and their leashes are donned. Outside at last, we retrace our paths around one or another block, romp through one or another field to retrieve and leave messages on all the canine answering machines posted throughout the neighborhood. After Walk there's Biscuit. After Biscuit, it's Drink, followed by Panting on the floor beside someone's feet, where, eventually, the condensation and moisture from each dog's nostrils and lips leave a damp butterfly on the hallway slates, distinct and curious as the signature Whistler painted on his canvases. Then it's Nap.

A few mornings ago, I realized that these small rituals extend even further. After Biscuits, when everyone has come inside, a few resident sparrows descend onto the porch stairs, where the dogs invariably crunch their treats. Overlooked by the dogs, and heretofore by me, the birds breakfast on the remaining crumbs.

Last night, the dogs awakened me to another cycle. Early spring, the last or next-to-last cold spell, we lit a fire to use up some of the nearly rotted wood that should have been burned winters ago. As always, the dogs curled up before the hearth. The progression I've watched so many times began: Dozing as close to the fire as we'll allow, then a head goes up and starts panting, then the backing-up walk that means "outside," then both of them go in the backyard for ten or fifteen minutes without us, then barking at the French doors that look in on the scene they'd just left to signal that it's time to come in and join us at the fireplace again. Inside, Outside, Inside, Outside—a dog's four seasons.

Along with the chill, the dogs' fur brings the smell of smoke back into the house—the very scent that the chimney's draft had efficiently vented from the room. But in the colder, moister, outdoor air, where the dogs have reexplored the yard for the umpteenth time today, the faint apple, burnt, resinous scents of our fire have been exchanged for the heat within their coats. Heat out, scent in: It's another biochemical cycle, like respiration or metabolism. As long as someone's willing to sit there by the fireplace, this comfort cycle continues: inside&warmth&fire then outside&cold&smoke.

Dogs awaken us to the comfort that familiarity brings with its cycles, patterns, routines, and seasons—rhythms we've all but given up, disguised or disregarded beneath the harried momentum of our scheduled lives. Yet participating in these seemingly insignificant nightly, weekly, and seasonal repetitions provides security and contentment to a social creature like a dog—like a human being. Just as those marked and remarked trees and fire hydrants ensure a dog's territory, the walks, biscuits, feedings, naps, games, fireplace sessions, and most reassuringly our entrances and exits, all provide pivotal moments throughout a day, around which the dogs wind the clock of their days (Milan Kundera's simile) as well as our own.

Someone once said that people invented time so that everything doesn't happen at once, and perhaps, before the advent of global networks and satellites and live coverage, it was possible to live a life one day at a time, one place at a time. But today, I'd argue, we need the dog's small acts of salvation to redeem us from the chaos of simultaneity and distraction. Dogs train us to savor a now, and then a now, and then a now again amid the overwhelming cacophony of obligations, good intentions, juggled appointments, and other self-important inventions that void our days of the harmony that repetition and fidelity bring. Dogs train us adults to play as children or dogs might play, with an unencumbered abandon that truly abandons the anxieties of an impossibly domesticated existence. To share in a dogmocracy, we give up our agendas, our grandiosity, and our rationalizing and live at least momentarily outside time, within the devoted realm of companionship. So to be with dogs is not suddenly to have all the time in the world but to have the world—or at least enough of it for the time being.

There's a wonderful creation story, retold in manifold variations through many cultures. In a Shawnee Indian version, the creator goes about finishing and perfecting each aspect of the world, followed always by her grandson and her dog. Even to this day, the little dog continues to accompany Our Grandmother, as the Shawnee call her. When souls ascend to the land of the dead, they come to a forked road; only one road leads to Our Grandmother. Good souls always choose correctly, while wicked souls never find her. As the good souls approach, they see Our Grandmother weaving a basket. Once she finishes it, the world will end: Into her basket, she will gather all the good souls to be saved for a new and better world, which they will repopulate; the wicked souls, however, will be lost forever. But each night, her little dog unravels all the weaving she has accomplished that day so that her work must continue and the world's end must wait until tomorrow.

Dog people know that to share a life with a dog is to have an ally in time-keeping (or is it time-losing?), an ally to unravel our all too tightly wound lives. *Revise, revise,* commands the fickle, driving human heartbeat. *Repeat, repeat,* entreats the dog's ticker—as does every other creature's on the planet. To lie next to a dog and stroke its fur is to resonate with another rhythm. (Did we need medical studies to tell us that petting a dog lowers stress levels and blood pressure?) Dog people have the comfort of at least some part of their lives that can be done over and over, again and again, without the anxiety of getting it right, rewriting, revising. A contented life for a dog is a repetition that holds no boredom or disappointment. Walk, Biscuit, Drink, Nap, and so many other happy recurrences—they're all positions on the face of a dog's natural clock. And even though each dog finally disappoints us with its death, we are the ones who call it untimely, wishing and willing the repetitions to outlast our longer lives.

This morning was Dog Bath, the lone ritual dogs would happily revise out of existence—all their hard work down the drain! Afterward, at a vigorous Brushing, I extract handfuls of hair from both coats: reddish blond and pale gold moss that compresses into one palm-size ball. I carry it across the yard that, despite the tufts of reviving grass and the daffodil leaves emerging from the vinca beds, still bears small mounds of snow, like islands from another season. Exactly four seasons ago, two nests hung low enough to the ground for me to peer into them, and there, among strips of our garden mulch, birds had interwoven tufts of the dogs' brushed hair—a furry, mammalian insulation for the eggs.

So this year, I toss the clumps of dog hair into the ivy as if I were sowing bird seeds into the air—seeds that will actually become birds. And although I cannot ensure this in any way, it makes me glad just to hope that some bird may knit these tufts into this ordinary backyard cycle, in which the dogs have included me.

Finally, a word about the less lucky dogs. Profits from *Dog People* help dog people and cat people whose animals are at risk of being given up or put down because of their own illness, age, or financial hardship. The Company of Animals Fund, which began in 1990 with the revenues from my first anthology, offers direct service grants to shelters and humane societies around the country. In plain terms, each copy of this book helps a dog or cat, working, as other humane efforts do, toward eliminating the problems caused by pet over-population. Unlike so many of society's woes, the problem of too many cats and dogs, too many euthanized cats and dogs, is solvable. Ironically, the solution does not require an apocalyptic discovery, enormous sum of money, or even the resolution of some highly politicized issue. The solution is individual responsibility. Education. Heroic, and mostly unheroic, generosity. *Dog People* provides a moment in which to give thanks—to the contributors to this book, to the volunteer shelter workers, and to each of you who has spayed or neutered your animals and taken the responsibility of this rare companionship to heart. For more information about the Fund, feel free to write to me in care of Artisan, 708 Broadway, New York, NY 10003.

Harry Sighing

Edward Albee

Those of us who have lived with Irish Wolfhounds—and I have shared lives with seven, once three of them with me at the same time, more often two—know that the nonsense about we humans being sole possessors of consciousness is exactly that. All seven of my Irish friends possessed a consciousness—awareness of self, awareness of selflessness, awareness of mortality—far more persuasive than that of many people I have known.

Interesting books have been appearing recently about the lives of dogs—their minds, their habits, their needs. These books range from the rather rudely clinical to the mawkishly anthropomorphic, but they all are interesting, at least to those of us who feel incomplete without the company of a dog or two, or more.

When I was a child, my family kept Dalmatians (at the stable where they also kept saddle horses), Pekingese (distaff family here, the asthmatic dogs kept either in upstairs sitting rooms or in the crook of arms), and an unhappy Saint Bernard, who became fat and lazy, for he didn't get to run much or sink deep in snow, or rescue anybody, or *anything*.

So . . . I grew up with dogs. There were cats, too, as I recall, but my family did not let them in the house, rather as if they were raccoons, or opossums. I have tried, over the years, to make it up to cats by having them everywhere—inside, outside, in my lady's chamber—discovering that dogs and cats coexist splendidly, especially if they are eating from the same bowl, so to speak.

It was not until my (theoretical) adulthood, however, that the Irish Wolfhound and I met across that crowded room, our eyes locking.

There are problems with Irish Wolfhounds, and I would not deny them. They are very large animals and they take up a good deal of space; they are fond of beds and couches, but if they can be persuaded not to usurp these, they will settle for floors, if the floor areas they settle for are close to human feet. Their deeply friendly nature expresses itself in great, swathing tail wags that can clear a table of bibelots in a second—a perfect argument against bibelots, of course. They have, as well, a great fondness for human food, and their height makes setting a buffet table hazardous. They will not put their paws up on the table and lean in, but if they are walking by and food is within reach, they assume it is there for them—and who is to say it is not? They are very fond of fruit, by the way; one of my dogs sat by pots of wild strawberries, waiting for the fruit to ripen; then he would nose in, carefully, and eat away. The greatest problem with Irish Wolfhounds, though, is that they don't live very long: their great hearts give out. A good deal of this is genetic, of course, but I think it is in part that they worry so for us, care so much.

And then there is the matter of the sighing.

Dogs bark; they whimper; they groan; they growl. But Harry sighed . . . a lot. Harry was the first Irish Wolfhound I shared my life with, and he lived the longest of them all, dying finally at twelve—very, *very* old for an Irish Wolfhound.

He was terribly arthritic toward the end and clearly in considerable discomfort, and the unhappy sounds he made—standing up, for example—were not the sighs that distinguished him; these were real groans: "Oh, God, not another day with bones like this!" And I am not certain of the sound he made when I told him Hubert Humphrey had died (Harry was a liberal Democrat); perhaps that was a *combination* of groan and sigh.

No, I mean the real sigh sounds he made—when we would be sitting together looking out at the ocean and I would say, "Aren't those great waves!?" and he would lean against me a little and just . . . sigh; or, when he would be stretched out (after a meal?), all thirty-seven yards of him, and I would say, "Happy?" and a great rumbling sound would escape his throat, a deeper, less ruminative sound, but a sigh nonetheless.

I was sitting reading one afternoon by my pool, and Harry was nearby—say, five feet away—and I happened to look over at him; he was staring off into some middle distance, prone, front paws crossed, and he just . . . sighed. This sigh was not a reply; it was Harry sighing to himself over something.

I miss him a great deal.

As long as I can remember, I've loved animals. As soon as I could walk, I'd scatter bread crumbs in the yard, then sit on my mother's lap and watch the animals eat. How I loved the silly, scampering squirrels, the bossy bluejays and timid sparrows.

When I was three, a majestic white cat showed up at our back door, and my mother let me keep him—much to the dismay of our neighborhood birds and squirrels, who became the object of his many hunting expeditions. But what a gentle creature he was with the family! His noble demeanor remained unchanged even when I picked him up by the throat or cut off all his long whiskers with Mother's scissors.

I suppose my becoming an artist was predestined. My mother was an artist, and her mother, and her mother before her. When I was two, my mother put a pencil in my hand, and I immediately started drawing animals. By the time I was in grade school, I knew I wanted to combine my talent for drawing with my love of animals to make animal portraiture my career.

When I was seven, I decided I wanted a dog. I had read all about dogs in the 1968 Encyclopædia Britannica my father had bought, and had carefully scrutinized the photos of the various breeds. I wanted either a Pekingese or a Pomeranian.

I begged. I pleaded. I cried. I drew countless pictures of dogs and plastered them all over the house as little reminders. I swore the puppy would be no trouble to my parents. That fall, when I fell off my bike and bloodied my mouth, my father presented me with a beagle—a stuffed one. I cried.

Four days before my eighth birthday, I was drawing in the sun parlor when I heard my father's car pull up. He was home early from work. I ran to the front window. There he was, getting out of his car in his rumpled gray raincoat, when he reached back in and picked up something tiny and black.

"Dad's home, and it looks like he's brought you another stuffed toy," my older sister, Eleanor, called to me from upstairs.

"No, it's not!" I cried. "It's a real dog!" Dad came in wearing a broad grin and placed the puppy on the floor. He was so small and wobbly he could hardly stand. I named him Pom Pom the Pomeranian.

As Mother instructed, we put him in a towel-lined box in the kitchen that night. But his high-pitched wails broke my heart. I sneaked downstairs and brought him up to my bed, where he slept every night for the next eighteen years.

I was true to my word and cared for Pom Pom myself. I fed

SELF-PORTRAIT WITH POM POM.

CHRISTINE HERMAN MERRILL
SAMANTHA.

17

CHRISTINE HERMAN MERRILL
SIR LANCELOT AND MAXIMILLAN.

CHRISTINE HERMAN MERRILL
TOP: HOMER AT MERRIDELL. BOTTOM: RALPH.

19

him, washed and brushed him, walked him. My eighth birthday fell on Easter, and Mother had the house brightly decorated with Easter baskets, Easter bunnies, and dyed eggs. I couldn't resist putting Pom Pom in an Easter basket centerpiece with yellow stuffing and colored eggs. So sweet and gentle, the Easter puppy just stayed there.

In September my parents separated, and a bitter divorce process began. Whenever I was sad or crying, Pom Pom would always come and nudge his nose under my hand and gaze at me with eyes as moist as mine. Sometimes, just to get away from the sadness of the house, I would give him rides in the deep basket of my bicycle. He loved to race into the wind, ears back, nose up, sniffing the scents of the neighborhood.

In my spare time I drew and painted Pom Pom in dozens of positions—in pencil, charcoal, oils. "Sleeping Pom Pom." "Frisky Pom Pom." "Wistful Pom Pom." It was easiest to sketch him when he was in a sound sleep. I would sit cross-legged, sketching him, then turn over a new page, move a few feet around him, and start a new sketch. Sometimes I even stood over him and sketched the aerial view.

I had always liked to sketch animals in unexpected positions, instead of the standard frontal view. I often sketched Pom Pom from behind, his head bent around looking back at me. By the time he was two, he had grown thick, white puffs on his hindquarters that almost trailed on the ground, and his curly, upturned tail sprouted long gray hair. I started experimenting with charcoal, to duplicate the rich range of grays. And through these early sketches of Pom Pom I tried to capture an animal's soul—roguish or relaxed, noble or playful.

When Pom Pom was twelve, I painted an oval oil portrait of him. His muzzle was tinged with white, which gave him a distinguished look. His brown eyes sparkled with compassion. Then I painted a self-portrait with Pom Pom in my arms. It hangs on my wall now. Sometimes I laugh when I look at it. Such a serious portrait, and the composition reminds me of a Madonna and Child. Since then, I have always enjoyed painting animals with their keepers, to show the close relationship between them.

When I left my childhood home for a house of my own, Pom Pom came with me. Toward the end, he couldn't see or hear very well and didn't walk around much, but he always seemed content. I coaxed him to eat and carried him from room to room so he could always be near me. One evening he passed away in his sleep, a painless ending so suited to his gentle soul.

Pom Pom lives in my paintings, in every pair of shining brown eyes I paint, in the curve of a tail, in the turn of a head. My mother taught me to paint, but if I am able to capture on canvas a dog's unique personality, his devotion, his warmth and joy, it's because of what Pom Pom taught me—the spiritual bond between a dog and a human family.

CHRISTINE HERMAN MERRILL
NORA.

21

CHRISTINE HERMAN MERRILL

MINNY.

CHRISTINE HERMAN MERRILL
TOP: JACKIE AND RUSSELL AT WHITE COLUMNS. BOTTOM: CHESS.

23

Gus and Dinah

Frederick Busch

Judy and I drove to our new teaching jobs in upper central New York, about 200 miles north of New York City, in a dark blue Corvair convertible. We carried distilled water for the iron, since we thought we were leaving civilization, and we carried a cake Judy had baked for my birthday, which we would celebrate that night, August 1, on the bare floor of the bare apartment we had rented. With us in the car, ears flapping and teeth grinning into the wind that made the Corvair shudder, was Gus, our year-old first Labrador.

Gus helped us celebrate my birthday that night. He also had helped to punctuate the unease that accompanies a big move by chasing the first car he saw in front of our house. He caught it and it stopped. He somehow sprained a paw and thereafter told the neighborhood of our arrival—it was very late at night—by yelping in an ecstasy of fright and woundedness. That night, the three of us noted my twenty-fourth birthday on the floor of a rented half-house, the furniture for which would come, perhaps, in the morning. Gus ate more of the icing than we did.

He was a wonderful big black dog, with a little soft-fleeced golden retriever in his background. We thought him, as most parents do their first child or surrogate, quite brilliant. We decided at last that he was a writer, perhaps a poet. He was also vindictive, and when we left him once for half a day, alone in the living room, he removed each of three cushions from our sofa, then tore away the lining of the sofa bench and removed every white, wooly wad of stuffing. The living-room floor looked like early snow.

Taking advice from local people, we fetched home a female Labrador who, we were told, would calm our temperamental male. We named her Dinah, and she was as low to the ground, stumpy, whip-tailed, and fixed on attending to us—pure Lab, in other words—as Gus was leggy and contemplative.

As they grew into dogdom together, Gus and Dinah acquired a routine. Most mornings, Judy went off to her teaching job at Madison Central School and I left to teach my eight o'clock class of conscripted freshmen. Gus and Dinah left too, for a day's work on the Colgate campus. Gus had no sense of direction that we could discern. He wandered as if lost, often, and we assumed he was either perceiving hard or composing about his perceptions. With Dinah on the scene, though, in all her raw bird-dogness, Gus's problems were solved. She headed down Lebanon Street to make a right on Broad and stroll the village green to the campus, and Gus let her lead. He tucked his head along her flank, and they went directly to wherever it was Dinah knew they ought to be. She was the creature of obligations and proprieties, and Gus was, well, he was thinking.

They went, usually, to Taylor Lake, an artificial lake on the edge of the green, hilly campus. We sneaked along on weekend mornings to learn their routine. Dinah made it known to students or faculty that it was her job and Gus's to return to the thrower any tossed object, preferably a stick that would float in Taylor Lake. She brought up the subject by delivering a good-sized piece of wood at the feet of the potential thrower. She stood rigidly, muscles quivering, as if on the verge of explosion.

When the stick was thrown, she followed it. Gus followed her.

At dinnertime, they arrived at the house, Dinah of course in the lead, ready for a meal.

She was also the more nervous about protecting us. We moved to a larger rental house in Hamilton, and we had a backyard. Judy, who loves to garden, knew that we would need a double length of garden hose. We were conscious of what a luxury we had somehow managed to afford, and Judy spent considerable time selecting two lengths of black, heavy hose. We returned with it one Saturday morning, from either Sears or Agway, and we laid it the length of the side driveway, thinking to connect it to the spigot later in the day. In our living room, sitting on the repaired but always lumpy little sofa we'd brought from New York, Judy heard a strange sound—a growling, a kind of tugging, a sound of combat. She asked Gus what he thought it was. He regarded her, checked with me, yawned in dismissal, and returned to his nap.

That afternoon, Judy called me from the house. She had no words. She pointed at the driveway. Dinah stood beside here, wagging hard: *See? I did it for you.*

Dinah had noted the serpent lying in a dangerous wait, and she had dispatched it. We were saved. The long black menace had been cut apart, sawed by the clean white teeth of a healthy Lab. It lay there, vanquished, in remarkably neat two-foot lengths.

There were generations of their puppies in yards and in dormitories. There were photographs in the student newspaper of Gus and Dinah plunging after sticks in Taylor Lake.

Our son Ben came along, and we bought a house in the country where Gus, who lasted longer, was guardian and retriever for Ben and then Nick. He was the resident poet of the house in Poolville.

Our next dog was suburban. We bought him while visiting a friend in Putnam County. We were talking about our current state of doglessness, and she urged upon us the local newspaper. We saw an ad for Labradors, and we—Judy and I and Ben and Nick—fell into instant motion, and were in the car and aiming for a certain downstate kennel. That was where we found Taxi. I named him that because I am from Brooklyn and because we'd just returned from several months in London, and I thought I'd enjoy, each night, calling his name over the cornfield near the Poolville house and evoking a fact of both cities. It was a bellow some of our neighbors never learned to appreciate, and the local dog inspectors were never even approximately charmed.

Taxi became a rural dog promptly enough, and his mission consisted of allowing children to play with and on him, and of killing snakes in Judy's garden with a fervor one associates with the mongoose.

In nearby Poolville Lake, where Judy and the boys were picnicking one afternoon, Taxi saw a deer in the brush. He made sounds of confusion and pursuit, and the deer leaped into the lake to swim for its life. Taxi followed, and he became part of our own wonderful version of Keats's urn: the deer forever in frantic retreat—doing, it would have to be said, a version of dog paddle and Taxi forever in pursuit to the tune of his panting and wet groans. We are required, by fondness and perversity, to once in a while wonder what he might have done had he caught the deer.

Now there are Junior and Jake. Taxi lived long enough to show the precincts to Jake, a small, purebred male who is the loyalest of friends. And Jake has in turn shown Junior, a year younger than he and a good deal larger, how to patrol the acres around the house where we now live, on a wild ridge above Sherburne, New York.

Jake is quite reminiscent of Dinah, and Junior is shaggy and not unlike Gus. It is Junior who eyes the hoses with Dinah's slightly mad glare, and it is Junior who has retrieved small rabbits and baby birds. Jake is awash in being dutiful. He delivers hurled sticks or balls with solemn urgency, while Junior, once he has retrieved them, is content to chew them into neat segments.

Each is a handsome, funny companion and each is our friend. And neither's the poet Gus was.

Bunny

Brian Hagiwara

Sometimes my bulldog Bunny reminds me of E.T. crossed with a stuffed teddy bear.

DISCOVERIES
Will Shively

I have always had dogs—mostly circus dogs (you know, the kind you get at the pound who learn to do dozens of tricks and become favorites of the entire neighborhood). But later, to appease the allergies of new family members, I bought a standard poodle.

Now I have three, all intelligent, but all black—eyes, nose, coats—and that makes them rather unphotogenic unless I yield and have them clipped into the puff-ball show clip.

So these are photographs of other people's dogs. With each animal I tried to reveal the essence or energy that identifies that particular dog or breed. A slower shutter speed permitted me to solidify those essential movements—which are usually too fast for anything but the camera's eye. Here are a few of the discoveries.

WILL SHIVELY

WILL SHIVELY

WILL SHIVELY

WILL SHIVELY

WILL SHIVELY

WILL SHIVELY

WILL SHIVELY

True Confessions

Susan Conant

I was raised to believe that souls were for Catholics and Baptists and that what Congregationalists got instead was character. Character required an awful lot of hard work. Souls felt effortless. They got cleansed and saved, presumably by Someone Else. When I was in the second grade, the Catholic girls got white First Communion dresses. *Bless me, Father,* they learned to whisper, *for I have sinned.* How I longed to restore the soul I didn't have! At my church, we learned about Jesus, whose love struck me as so oddly unconditional it was hard to believe that Congregationalists got Him. God's love was like my own father's: contingent, elusive, capricious. We sang hymns: "Work, for the night is coming, work through the morning hours. . . ."

Souls weren't in evidence at home, either. My mother thought they were a religious version of plastic lamp shade covers, overplucked eyebrows, and *True Confessions* magazine. My father worshiped dogs, hunting, fishing, the state of Maine, and the complete works of William Shakespeare, in that order. My mother loathed dogs, hated hunting and fishing, refused to move to Maine, and habitually misquoted Shakespeare. My parents' marriage was not a union of soul mates. Perhaps that's the real reason they avoided the topic.

So I didn't learn about souls until I was in the seventh grade and found myself seated right behind Vinnie D'Angelo. I had a wild crush on Vinnie, who, in an act of Christian charity—amazing grace!—allowed me to drill him on his catechism. And that's where I first saw souls. The catechism was illustrated. One drawing was titled, as I recall, "The Catholic Church Is the Stairway to Heaven." The picture showed a flight of steeply rising steps. What Heaven looked like I don't remember. My attention was fixed on the two souls that hadn't got there yet. The big black blot never would. The other, white, of course, wafted upward. If there'd been such things as Congregationalist souls, they'd have had to lumber up step by step. Even so, I had a sense of fascinated relief. I treated the catechism as a sort of Peterson guide to metaphysical entities. If a soul ever flew by, now at least I'd spot its field marks.

I had to wait a long time. Meanwhile, mainly because of dogs, I scraped by with character. Ah, family values—meaning, in my family, those of the paterfamilias. Presented with a .22, I was a decent shot, but refused to aim at living things. I repeatedly lost my father's hand-tied dry flies to treetops; the only leafless thing I ever hooked was the part of the state of Maine that lies at the bottom of the Dennys River. Whenever the prospect of moving to Maine arose, I found myself in unsettling agreement with my mother. Shakespeare was a lot of work. Thank God for dogs—as loving as Jesus and almost as effortless as Catholic souls. And, of course, when it comes to building character, a dog is as good as hard work. So my father believed. My mother didn't, but then she disagreed with him about everything, and, as I've mentioned, she loathed dogs.

I grew up in the shadow of a legend, a New England Field Trial Champion of the late thirties and the great dog of my father's life, Lexington Milligan Jock. According to the dates, my parents must have met while my father was actively campaigning Jock, and my father was not a person who considered any dog, never mind his prize pointer, some sort of incidental possession like a first edition of a rare book or fluency in an obscure language that might not happen to drift into the conversation. On the contrary, he talked about dogs all the time and always took his own dogs everywhere. I can only conclude that the legendary Jock fooled my mother into mistaking him for something other than what he was, perhaps a liver-and-white-ticked chair or an oddly hairy person.

Jock's puppies did not take her in. There were two litters, both whelped shortly before my birth. When my mother died, the only piece of dog memorabilia she left was a clipping of a classified ad that she placed when I must have been a few months old. It reads: "My husband's fifty-dollar puppies for twenty-five dollars. If a man answers, hang up." My father kept two puppies, Jock's Great Stuff and Jock's Little Nonsense. Stuffy was the pick puppy. Nonny was so clearly the runt of both litters that no one wanted her, even at half-price, until I was old enough to bid. She barked at strangers and shook like Jell-O.

When I was three years old, the polio epidemic offered my father the opportunity to acquire a new piece of the state of Maine while simultaneously moving human beings out of his life. He gave my mother a log cabin on a Maine lake and insisted that she take me there every summer to get me out of the disease-ridden city. The dogs came along. Stuffy and Nonny and I rode in the backseat of the car. I slept on them. In those days, dogs smelled like dogs. Our car did too. So, undoubtedly, did I. No one ever shampooed the dogs. Since the cabin had no bathtub, I bathed in the lake. So did the dogs. Every day, Stuffy swam a half-mile across and back. Only years later did I learn his destination: a summer camp where the boys fed him doughnuts.

In those days, dogs and children ran loose. Dogs lost their freedom only if they bit people. Ours didn't. Nonny sometimes tried but was always yanked away by my irate mother, who would astonish Nonny's intended victims by vehemently taking their side. The dogs were her husband's, she would explain; if it were up to her, she wouldn't give the damned things house room. Stuffy never tried to bite anyone. On the contrary, he went out of his way to ingratiate himself with everyone, especially my mother, to whom he was devoted. Stuffy was what I would now call an alpha male. As a puppy, he'd been the first out of the whelping box and had eaten the kibble meant for the entire litter. In fact, his original name was Hitler. In playing up to my mother, perhaps he sought *Lebensraum.* In the face of his advances on her, she was London during the blitz.

It is now clear to me that she was afraid of dogs. My father maintained that she didn't understand them. What she failed to grasp, he argued—one more principle he still hadn't drummed into her head—was that a dog is always going to act like a dog. *That,* said my mother, was exactly what she didn't like about them—that and the fact that no matter how much she tried to keep them away, they were inexplicably attracted to her. Cats were too, or so my mother always insisted. She hated cats almost as much as she hated dogs. It has occurred to me that what she actually disliked were living things. At any rate, what my mother viewed as her animal magnetism was strikingly unobservable whenever she called the dogs or, indeed, tried to get them to do anything at all. I have a vivid memory of a hot summer afternoon spent at a Howard Johnson's on the Maine Turnpike. My mother had let the dogs out of the car, and Stuffy had taken off. She wouldn't have dared to leave without him. I now see that she was even more afraid of my father than she was of dogs; she had even less ability to control his behavior than theirs. She and Nonny and I waited all afternoon for Stuffy to return. He always came back. He was hit by cars a few times but lived until he and I were both thirteen. For two dogs, we had one leash. It was almost never used.

For two malamutes, I own dozens: show leads, leather leads in six-foot, four-foot, and two-foot lengths; nylon leashes in bright colors with training collars to match; longe lines; retractable leads; traffic tabs. I own two X-back harnesses, a sled, and two skijoring outfits I've never had the guts to try. If there's a way to fasten myself to a big, muscular wolf-gray dog with a blocky muzzle, good ears, a stand-off coat, and a tail carried high, like a plume waving, I own it, or if I don't own it today, I'll buy it tomorrow. I never deliberately turn a dog loose. A few days ago, Kobi escaped; he slipped by my husband, who isn't the old fox with dogs that I am. My husband and I have worked out a system to get the dogs to do what he wants: He tells me, and I tell the dog. The scheme works very well. Two minutes after Kobi had vanished, my husband was handing me a leash and a fistful of dog food, and telling me where Kobi had gone. When I hollered, Kobi did a perfect recall, straight front and all. My heartbeat was audible for an hour afterward. The incident happened not on the Maine Turnpike but at the end of a suburban street that goes from nowhere to nowhere. How Stuffy survived, I do not know.

My parents' marriage did not, or not exactly. My father lived to eighty-eight, my mother to seventy-eight. For the last twenty-five years, they never saw or even spoke to each other, but they never divorced. My mother thought that divorce was in bad taste. She continued to use my father's name; she was Mrs. Paterfamilias. When my father retired, he moved to Maine in search of his soul. He should have got a dog. Instead, he discovered vodka. He gave up fishing. He brandished handguns but did not hunt. Shakespeare endured. Dead drunk, deeply paranoid, his brain pickled, his hip joints eaten away by alcohol, his hearing and eyesight gone, my father never misquoted. As he often reminded me, those decades were the winter of his discontent. Visiting my father during one of his stints in a geriatric-psychiatric ward, I heard all about a Samoyed that had been there the day before, a remarkable dog, according to my father, a fascinating creature that had performed tricks. I visited my father seldom and wrote often. My letters were almost exclusively about dogs.

When my mother moved out of the house I grew up in, she sold a sterling silver challenge trophy that Jock had retired, a big bowl with the names of dogs engraved on it, Jock's the only name to appear three times. I wish I'd been offered the right of first refusal; I'd have paid anything for that silver bowl. Only after my mother died did I discover that she'd thrown away the photograph taken of my father and Jock the day they won that trophy. She was very angry at my father, and, of course, she hated dogs.

When my father died last November, my mother did not attend the funeral. She was old and frail, and she lived far from Dennysville, Maine, where years before he'd bought a cemetery plot at the top of a hill above the river he loved. At the end of the graveside service, I poured the water of the Dennys on the ground. Only four people attended: my husband and I, and a young couple who had been kind to my father. Among other things, for podiatric rather than religious reasons, they had washed his feet. My mother would not have belonged at the funeral. She wouldn't have known who it was we were burying. In her mind, my father was still young. I came very close to taking an Alaskan malamute to my father's funeral. As it was, Kobi waited in the car. Foolish, really. After all, the

obsequies took place outdoors, and if Kobi had lifted his leg on a headstone, there would have been almost no one there to see. Besides, my father would have been the last person to object to the presence of any dog, anytime, anywhere, including at his own open grave.

When I told my mother that my father had died, she seemed to have difficulty comprehending the reality of his death. Almost immediately, however, her chronic illness became acute. She died three months later. By then, my husband and I had two dogs, Kobi and a new puppy, Kobi's half-sister, another beautiful malamute, also dark wolf gray. I didn't consider taking either or both to my mother's funeral. Even if she had liked dogs or made an exception in the case of mine, she'd have considered the eccentricity in bad taste. Besides, the funeral was held indoors, in the same church where I'd learned about love and sung about hard work. The Bible passages I selected were those that had been read over my father's casket. I am a person of strong character: I gave my parents the same funeral. For obvious reasons, however, I assume that my father and mother have gone to different heavens.

Despite this true confession, I am still not Catholic. In fact, my principal religious belief is a conviction that the Alaskan malamute is the stairway to heaven. But I did spot the field marks on the soul when it finally arose. At first it looked like that big black blot doomed to spend eternity at the bottom of the stairs. Gradually, it has taken shape, acquiring the form of a large sled dog with a blocky muzzle, good ears, heavy bone, a stand-off coat, and a tail carried high, like a plume waving. Its color is neither black nor white, but dark wolf gray. It is the color of my own dogs.

THE CITY OF DOGS
Robert Andrew Parker

Nine years ago I was teaching in Amsterdam at the Gerrit Rietveld Academy. I had plenty of time for myself and I walked and walked. It was four miles from my house to the Academy, and I never used the train or the same route, so I saw a lot of Amsterdam. After a few days of this, I realized that the city really belonged to the dogs. They had complete liberty. They were everywhere and they were adored. I imagined what the city would be like without humans; how it would look and how it would run. These dogs are clergy.

ROBERT ANDREW PARKER
LEFT: BURGERS. CENTER: GEORGE. RIGHT: AN ACTOR.

ROBERT ANDREW PARKER
POSTLIBERATION DOGS AT KHAJURAHO.

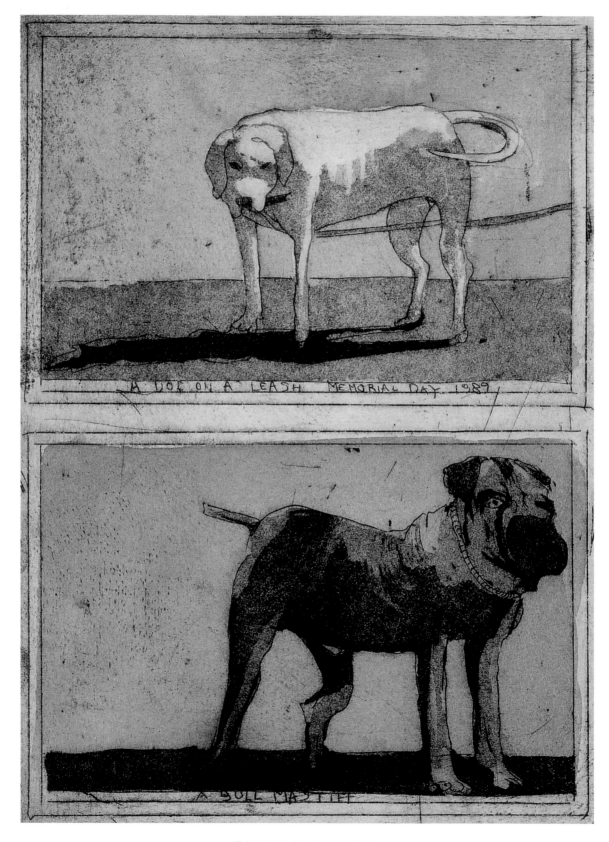

ROBERT ANDREW PARKER

TOP: A DOG ON A LEASH. BOTTOM: A BULL MASTIFF.

ROBERT ANDREW PARKER
BULLDOGS.

43

ROBERT ANDREW PARKER
A GAME LIKE CHESS.

THINKING OF SHEILA IN INDIA

ROBERT ANDREW PARKER
THINKING OF SHEILA IN INDIA.

45

Considerations (in Middle Age) Concerning Getting a Dog

Ann Beattie

A note to the reader: A dog isn't part of my everyday life anymore. I love dogs—at least, I tend to love dogs—but somehow the problems my houseplants have presented in recent years have made me reluctant to take on anything else that requires being considered when I travel, as well as a lot of water. Everybody else can water their plants once a week. Me: I have to water and mist daily, or they keel over. Still, there are those lonely moments when I'd love to hear the click-click of little doggie toenails, rather than the rustle of dead plant leaves hitting the floor. It's odd to have had a dog and then to be without one. The real truth is, I so loved my late great dog that I'm afraid another one might be a letdown. It's not that I don't think of it. Like other writers I know, I'm a haunted creature. Moments with the dog come back to me, and I see them in slow motion. I see them metaphorically. Worse yet are the many times I see them distinctly, without

any writerly perspective, and I have to confront the fact that I used to have something I don't have anymore. I am easily preoccupied with the should I/shouldn't I question. And when I least expect it, dogs creep into my consciousness. In the following scenarios, I will (also like other writers) give you a sense of *me,* while also making a few remarks about dogs, and the possibility they hold for changing everything.

1. "Let's see. Where did Ann put the baking powder? Baking soda, I see, but that wouldn't be a good substitute. Has to be in here somewhere, because when I cleaned this shelf a year ago, I know I put it . . . probably all the way to the back, the morning I was so mad that the muffins didn't rise. The whole pan of 'em acted like I'd put in baby powder instead of baking powder, rose about as high as your average unfolded diaper. Well: Always a surprise to find even more gourmet mustard than you ever thought you had.

'With hot, hot jalapeño and shiitake mushrooms.' Another of those weird but inexpensive gifts to bring the hostess, along with vinegars with all that odd stuff stuck in the bottle: vinegar with salmon skeleton, for example. Look at that! More of Paul Newman's spaghetti sauce, and I could have sworn we'd run out. But why is the jar lying on its side? Aah: knocked over by a large rodent cavorting through the cupboard, no doubt. How big would something have to be to knock over a fairly large bottle of spaghetti sauce? What to make for dinner . . . what to make."

HOW SITUATION WOULD BE IMPROVED BY THE PRESENCE OF A DOG: *I would be talking to the dog, not myself. Upon hearing "dinner," the dog would beat its tail in an encouraging way.*

2. "I am never going to be happy again. My talent has left me. I tried to write a simple description of a man walking across the floor, and I couldn't even think what a floor looked like. I mean it: I got hung up describing a rug that was a horrible rug, no rug I'd ever seen, and then I took the rug away and made it a bare floor, but I couldn't envision the wood. Oak? Was it an oak floor? And was this really essential to my story? I was closing my eyes, trying to imagine a floor—I mean, when I was a kid, at least I had the imagination to close my eyes and imagine myself a beautiful princess, but there I was, on a beautiful, sunny day, shut up in my writing room, trying to envision a floor that wasn't so spectacular it would stop the action, but that wasn't just an old, scuffed oak floor, and meanwhile, every thought my character was supposed to have went out of my mind, so then I had a silent character and no reason to send him

across the floor in the first place. This is the oddest, most frustrating activity. A grown woman, trying to envision and describe a floor."

HOW SITUATION WOULD BE IMPROVED BY THE PRESENCE OF A DOG: *Dog would walk back and forth across real floor as I paced, companionably, finding this discussion as interesting as any other, listening for magic word that would indicate all my thoughts were directed to him. ("Just an old, scuffed oak floor OUT ALPO EAT DON'T CHASE CARS.")*

3. I am asked to do a benefit reading for EWWW (Educated Writers Wanting Wealth). I am not able to think fast enough. I agree to do the reading. Afterward there is a buffet dinner, during which people come up to the writers as they are trying to dish up food. They enthusiastically touch the writers on their elbows, causing noodles to fall to the floor instead of slithering onto the plates, causing server to think writers are, predictably, drunk. Straddling dropped noodles, as Educated Writer explained personal lack of luck in the marketplace, I nod and sympathize. Then I am commended for writing the person's favorite book, *The Accidental Tourist*.

HOW SITUATION WOULD BE IMPROVED BY THE PRESENCE OF A DOG: *The dog is waiting in the car. When I try to help the waitperson scoop up the spilled noodles, saying they'll be perfectly fine for my dog, aforementioned waitperson will go off to the kitchen, thinking me, predictably, a starving writer, and, as I leave, press upon me an entire casserole, complete with Pyrex baking dish, for "the dog." I will later split it with the dog, while thinking over the evening and resolving to keep my phone on "voice control" at all times and, predictably, having a stiff drink.*

4. An enormous storm comes up, blowing a shutter off the house and further shattering a pane of glass previously shot through by some little monster's BB gun. Can't close the screens in time! Furniture soaked! Glass everywhere! That lightning—would it possibly hit the house?

HOW SITUATION WOULD BE IMPROVED BY THE PRESENCE OF A DOG: *Big game. At some point, pissed, wet, and frightened, I would look down and see the dog, happily accompanying me on the race-from-room-to-room game, panting happily, tail raised hopefully. I would see that this, like most other things, is ludicrous, and that I am ludicrous, besides. Or: Dog, frightened, would actually piss, shivering in the wetness, scared out of its mind. I would see that the dog is worse off than me, throw my arms around freaked-out dog, thinking, Well, at least I understand this is only a storm. Dogs often allow owners several seconds of momentary superiority.*

5. This is true: Every summer, for a week or so, we baby-sit our friends' dog, Sandy. The dog is a golden retriever, quite a nice fellow, one who wears his heart on his paw and all that. The dog enjoys riding in '68 Mustang convertible so much that he often runs into the garage and sits hopefully in the backseat. We take the dog to the beach and people who otherwise ignore us come up and talk pleasantly. "You mean you've never written anything about Sandy?" Rachel (eleven) says to me, as her brother Rob (eight) looks at me expectantly. "Well," I explain lamely, "we have pictures of Sandy on the refrigerator." But why wouldn't I write about Sandy? Chivalrous; sense of humor; devoted; sleek of coat; bright of eye. I mean, my husband makes pancakes for Sandy with his initial pressed in with M&M's, so wouldn't I, a writer, at least write about Sandy?

HOW SITUATION WOULD BE IMPROVED BY THE PRESENCE OF SANDY: *Rob and Rachel would think that here was an adult smart enough to know that Sandy was an exceptional dog. I could make fun of my husband, who sometimes finds Sandy's slavish devotion a bit much. He says to the dog: "Sandman—get a life." Often, when I make fun of my husband, magazine editors find the pieces funny and publish them and give me money. Sandy and my husband, Lincoln: There's a subject to run with.*

6. The day is sunny, beautiful. All my obligations are met. The flowers are blooming.

HOW SITUATION WOULD BE IMPROVED BY THE PRESENCE OF A DOG: *Anxiety can be displaced onto dog. First, look for ticks; next, put dog in lap and bury nose in his side. Wait for clouds to appear. The mail to come. The flowers to be buzzed by bees.*

Ooshi
Vladimir and Evgenia Radunsky

This is our dog named Ooshi,
who's constantly dreaming of sushi.

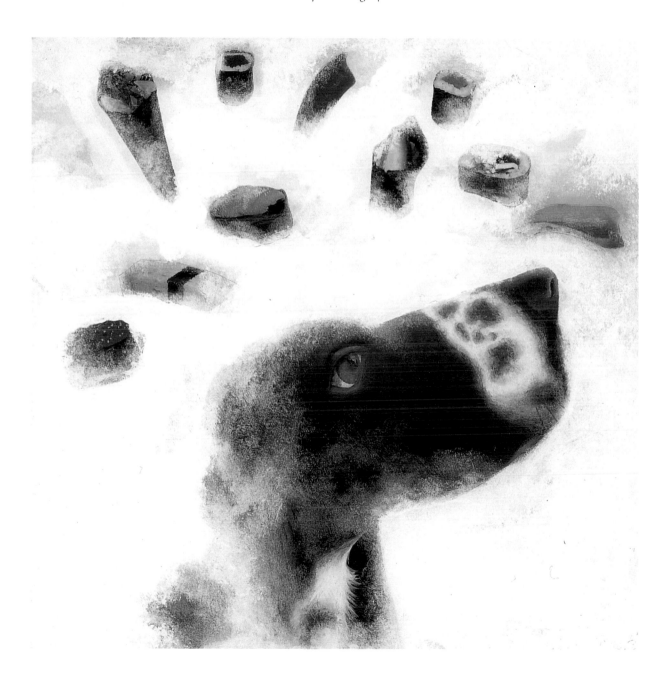

A Dog in Love

Merrill Markoe

Everyone remembers their first love. It is a very special and yet in some ways kind of frightening time—all those new and powerful feelings. Which is why, when I first observed my smallest dog, Winky, in the throes of a continuous passionate entanglement with my dog-shaped bedroom slipper (who among us can claim to have chosen wisely that first, heady time?), I felt some kind of a parental counseling session was in order. So I lifted him up from where he was stationed in the kitchen doing what he usually is doing—moving slowly from one side of the room to the other, licking the floor—and sat him down on the couch with me for a little chat.

*

ME: Winky, Winky, Winky, oh Winky. . . .

WINKY: Yes?

ME: You are getting to be a "big boy" now, not big in physi-

cal stature, because genetically you're some kind of a Shih Tzu deal, but in the biggest sense of the word, by which I mean—

W: What's your point exactly? I'd like to get back to licking the floor.

ME: Well, lately I couldn't help but notice that you are having your first intimate relationship, which to you probably feels very intense, very serious. . . . Please stop licking the couch like that. You're making saliva spots.

W: There are cheese molecules over by the back cushions.

ME: My point is that when someone, in this case you, has very strong positive feelings like you seem to be having lately for that shoe of mine, it's an emotion we call "love." Which is why I say, for example, I "love" you.

W: Is it time for dinner yet?

ME: No, it's 9:00 in the morning.

W: And what time is dinner?

ME: About 5:00, 5:30. About eight hours from now.

W: EIGHT HOURS??? You're joking.

ME: Forget about that for just a moment. I want to talk to you about this very special time in your life because there are certain dangers, certain pitfalls that perhaps I can help you avoid.

W: Eight hours? Isn't that cruel? If I called the Humane Society, wouldn't they threaten to take me away?

ME: According to veterinary charts and the American Kennel Club, you are just about double your appropriate weight.

W: Oh, but you're perfect. You open the refrigerator door about sixty times a day. You're *always* eating.

ME: Okay, okay. Listen to me for a minute.

W: That's seven minutes to me.

ME: Love can be a very powerful experience. You may find yourself awash in feelings you've never had. When I was a girl of about fourteen, though now that I think back, perhaps the most intense first love hit when I was in my twenties. . . .

W: You can't compare that situation to mine. Your shoe and I have an incredible chemistry.

ME: That's exactly my point. The first time it hits you, you don't understand that chemistry and love are not exactly the same thing.

W: You just don't like to *share* anything, do you? Just like with the food portions.

ME: I don't like to share? You guys share *everything* with me. Every room in my house, every piece of furniture.

W: And this is just the way you were acting when Lewis was dating the couch. Suddenly the battle lines are drawn.

ME: This isn't about battle lines. Lewis totally wrecked that couch. I was concerned that Lewis was a batterer. I am pleased to see at least you are far gentler with my shoe.

W: You can't compare Lewis and the couch to me and the shoe. Two totally different kinds of relationships.

ME: You're the one who made the comparison. The point I wanted to make is that, as with Lewis and the couch, these things don't always end happily. Lewis destroyed that couch, I had to have it hauled away. And that's the way it is with love. A lot of times one party gets hurt.

W: Well, I knew he was playing with fire. How stupid do you have to be to get sexually involved with a *couch*???

ME: Anyway, I just wanted to caution you to go more slowly. Don't rush things. Take your time. If there's anything I've learned in life it's that there's no real good side to romantic obsession.

W: Eight hours *must* be up by now. Let's go get something to eat.

INSIDE/OUTSIDE
William Wegman

Inside we enjoy....

sitting around

EXIT

OUT

Thinking about going out

parlor games

hiding

WILLIAM WEGMAN

53

WILLIAM WEGMAN

WILLIAM WEGMAN

In maine
we often
go fishing
in the canoe

swimming

on the other boat

isn't she yawl!

DOG BASEBALL

biking

or

or just sniffing around

fay takes up more than her share of
the couch

whereever she goes

(Sometimes I'll intercede on
the other dogs behalf)

WILLIAM WEGMAN

WILLIAM WEGMAN

Bird-Dogging

Deirdre McNamer

On the occasional blue-and-gold October day, my father would decide to go out and kill something. He wasn't much of a hunter, but shooting pheasants seemed like something a man should do in Montana, out there on the prairie where we lived.

He couldn't take our maybe-part-collie dog, Pansy, to flush the birds for him, because Pansy's stray-dog past had rendered her an abject coward with no skills. Pansy knew this, and she felt bad about herself. Sometimes she felt so bad she found a wad of discarded pink bubble gum, chewed it thoughtfully for a while, then wiped it all over her black forelegs.

So Pansy stayed home, and my father conscripted me and three younger siblings to be his bird dogs. Our job was to run along the borrow pit in close formation, barking furiously. If we happened to scare up a pheasant, we then had to run back up the road as fast as we could and take up positions *behind* our shotgun-wielding parent. Then he would fire mightily. By this time, the pheasant had made a dozen farewell phone calls, smoked a cigarette, and ambled away bored.

On my eighth birthday, I opened my presents—a fringed leather jacket and a five-year diary that locked with a miniature key—then joined my brother and sisters to go bird-dogging with Dad. Maybe it was because it was my birthday and I was feeling my position as the oldest of the dogs. But I remember tearing down the gravel road that day, fringes flying, yapping in that particular, frantic way you do when you are saying good-bye to one of your lives.

We flushed a big, bright pheasant. We ran back to take up our positions. The gun boomed. The bird, to our pure amazement, ruffled down dead.

"Dad shot a peasant today!" I wrote in my blank new diary, trying to make a dramatic, if not a dictionary-perfect, debut. "I got peasant blood on my new jacket! Pansy smelled it and ran away. I'm horse from barking. We barked all day. All day we were dogs."

Dawg-Eat-Dawg

If royal academies had football teams, my dog Clyde would have made one a splendid mascot. Even when he slobbered, Clyde had a certain patrician air about him, a look of world-weary resignation one associates with good breeding and disdain for the foibles of the lower orders. Raising his nose haughtily, he'd dodge and dart through underbrush with heavy-footed grace. Clyde would only lower his snout to search for a scent, and even then he'd maintain a kind of cool dignity: sniff, sniff, snuffle, snuffle, schnozzle, schnozzle, all nose and no nonsense.

Alas, in this era of sensitivity to animal rights, fewer and fewer pooches are enlisted to sniff and snuffle and schnozzle along the gridiron sidelines. My own college, Antioch, had no sports, much less mascots. Irony it had in abundance. To protest other schools' spending more for athletics than for academics, we rallied around a brussels sprout. Not since Dan Quayle was named captain of the DePauw University golf team had a vegetable been so exalted.

The brussels sprout's poise and physical toughness make it an ideal mascot. But it hardly inspires the fierce loyalty dogs do. Hundreds of humans gathered a few years back in Athens, Georgia, as UGA (pronounced "ugga") IV (pronounced "the fourth") was laid to rest in the University of Georgia's Sanford Stadium. "It was just something respectful, to perpetuate UGA IV's memory," says Frank (Sonny) Seiler, the dog's former master. Seiler watched as the red-and-black plywood coffin was carried by. "We didn't feel any religious ceremony was necessary."

Aside from King Tut, whom we'll deal with later, and perhaps Jimmy Hoffa, UGAs I, II, III, and IV are the most famous mammals to be buried within a football stadium. The white English purebreds are sealed in wall vaults just at the west end zone of the stadium, their epitaphs inscribed on their red Georgia marble crypts. UGA I's reads:

> UGA
>
> A REAL GEORGIA BULLDOG
>
> GEORGIA MASCOT
>
> (1956–1967)
>
> "DAMN GOOD DOG"

UGA the First followed in the pawprints of a couple of brindled bulldogs, the first named Butch and the second, Mike. UGA II claimed two SEC titles, and UGA III the 1980 national championship. But UGA IV was particularly mourned because he was Georgia's winningest mascot. His teams were 77-27-4 and went to a bowl in each of his nine seasons. Before opening kickoffs, UGA IV would be pulled to the fifty-yard line in a larger-than-life red fireplug, from which he emerged to dart across the field to his climate-controlled doghouse on the sidelines. With his loose skin and mournful face, he looked like a worried Old Testament prophet.

UGA the Wise was hounded by all sorts of civic groups. He served as chairdog of the American Cancer Society's Great American Smokeout in 1984. He did testimonials for the March of Dimes and volunteer work for the Humane Society. He accompanied Herschel Walker to the 1982 Heisman Trophy banquet, in Manhattan. On that occasion, UGA IV forsook his usual letter sweater for a white collar and black bow tie.

About the only places he avoided were flea markets. "UGA IV was the featured speaker at meetings of many of the various Bulldog Clubs," says Swann Brannon,

Seiler's daughter. He had a splendid voice that rumbled forth *basso profundo* when he addressed large convocations, a talent that might have made Georgia president Charles Knapp envious. That and the fact that the UGAs rate one more page than Knapp does in the Bulldog media guide.

Of course, not everyone is gaga over UGA. "The only reason Georgia even has a bulldog mascot is that the school was founded by a bunch of Yale missionaries," snarls Chris Getman, the keeper of Handsome Dan XIII, Yale's bulldog. "Dan puts UGA to shame. As far as I can tell, UGA just sits on the sidelines and sweats." Dan can stand on his hind legs, jump through a Hula Hoop, and sink to the bottom of a pond. Asked if he would rather go to Harvard or die, he plops to the ground, rolls over, and plays dead.

According to Yale historians, Dan XIII carries on the oldest official line of college mascots in the U.S.: the Dan Dynasty is now celebrating its 105th anniversary—735th, in dog years. The original Handsome Dan was bought from a New Haven blacksmith for five dollars. He led Eli football teams to 125 victories in 131 games and inspired Cole Porter, class of '13, to write "Bulldog," a song still howled whenever Yalies gather together.

When Handsome I died in 1898, *The Hartford Courant* wrote: "He was always taken to games on a leash, and for years the Harvard football team owed its continued existence to the fact that the rope held." Actually, the first Dan is still around. Like Lenin, he was stuffed and preserved behind glass. He presides over the trophy room in the Yale gym.

No successor was crowned until twenty-five years later, when the ignominious reign of Dan II began. That Dan was kidnapped on the eve of the 1934 Harvard-Yale football game and photographed licking the hamburger-smeared boots of John Harvard's statue. Yale won 14-0, but the humiliation was never forgotten. "The crew team went so far as to adopt its own bulldog, creating a canine Great Schism," wrote Elliot Tannenbaum, a noted Danographer. "Dan was shunned by the campus community until he broke his leg and died three years later, unloved and unmourned."

Getman calls No. 13 Maurice, after Ron Maurice Darling, the former Yale pitcher now in the major leagues. When Darling was a sophomore, Getman hired him to paint his house. "Ron painted all the windows shut," Getman says. "This is my revenge." A bluff, barrel-chested New Haven financial consultant, Getman is living proof that alumni come to look like their mascots. The main difference between Getman and Dan is that Getman seldom drools in public.

Dan XIII has lunched with George Bush, '48, and corresponds with Millie, the former First Pooch. In the dog days of summer, he vacations on the Jersey shore. And though it never made the society pages of *The New York Times,* Dan was once affianced to a greyhound (the dog, not the bus).

Yet he's no Fancy Dan. In fact, he's a bit of a hot dog. He has chased Princeton cheerleaders into the stands and was once kicked out of a Harvard game for assaulting a mounted policeman.

The UGAs tend to be more submissive. UGA IV was slapped down by the Baylor bear and bayed at by Smokey, the blue tick coonhound of the Tennessee Volunteers. UGAs are also more circumspect. IV once showed his distaste for South Carolina by leaving a memento in the Gamecock end zone during the national anthem.

Both dynasties have been dogged by injuries. Dan XIII nearly wound up as roadkill a few years back, when he narrowly escaped assassination by a car he may or may not have been chasing. UGA IV tore a ligament in his left hind leg after jumping off a hotel bed. What a bulldog was doing in a hotel bed is anybody's guess.

John Saunders finds that episode distasteful, much like bulldogs themselves. "They don't live long, are difficult to breed, and have lots of potential genetic defects," he snaps. "Salukis have none."

Saunders ought to know. He ministers to Tut II, the saluki mascot of Southern Illinois. The Afghan-like Tut II lives in a veritable shrine of salukiness: Saunders's home is crammed with saluki sculptures, saluki paintings, even saluki switch plates. Tut II sleeps on a water bed and watches TV with a three legged poodle named Muffy.

Tut II, Saunders asserts, has a nobler lineage than either Dan or UGA. Salukis were the royal dogs of Egypt. Southern Illinois's first saluki, King Tut, is entombed under a concrete pyramid at McAndrew Stadium, about fifty yards from the north goalpost.

No doubt Tut and several generations of Dans and UGAs now frolic at the gate to the underworld with Cerberus, the multiheaded mutt of a god named Pluto.

Canine Company
Jamie Wyeth

My great problem is that I would rather be in the company of nonhumans. I mean, given my druthers, I would choose aloneness. But if accompanied, I would choose a pig, a sea gull, or a dog. As a consequence, the major body of my work is paintings of individual creatures, furred or feathered. As this is a book of dogs, my contribution will be of my furred subjects, and in keeping with my lifelong belief, I will let my work speak for me. Herewith is a painting collection of subjects that meant and mean an awful lot to me.

BOOM BOOM IN WINTER.

JAMIE WYETH
TOP: KLEBERG—ASLEEP AND AWAKE.
BOTTOM: KLEBERG.

JAMIE WYETH

JAMIE WYETH
TREE DOG.

A Walk with Jacques

Daniel Pinkwater

As I write this, Jacques, a ninety-pound, tawny, shepherd-type dog is snoozing at one end of the old leather couch in my office. If I were to rise from my chair, Jacques would open an eye. Were I to reach for my coat, he'd be on his feet, crowding me a bit, lest I forget to take him with me. He hopes we'll go to our park. It's not a park in the conventional sense; it's better—it's the beautifully landscaped grounds of the Vanderbilt Mansion National Historic Site, in Hyde Park, New York, just a few minutes' drive from my house.

For years now, Jacques and I have done a brisk mile or two nearly every morning. We leave the parking lot and go north for a half-mile. The path takes us along the top of a high ridge, the Hudson River below us. Sometimes there are deer in the sloping meadow between us and the river. We may see a hawk and, rarely, an eagle. At the turnaround point, Jacques pees. We then walk the half-mile back to the car. If we're doing the short walk, Jacques pees again as we approach the parking lot.

In the two-mile routine, we pass the mansion, go halfway around the circular drive, observe the astonishing beech trees, turn back, and stop at two symmetrical bushes, where Jacques pees. If we feel like it, we may do the whole thing over again. We nod to other walkers encountered on the path. When we meet another dog, Jacques, who loves all dogs, makes an urgent, moaning noise, *sotto voce,* but he never breaks pace or moves away from his position at my left side. When we return to the car, Jacques gets a biscuit.

When we get home, Jacques is likely to nuzzle my hand before we go about our individual tasks. (Usually I go to my desk and Jacques to his couch, for another of the naps in which he specializes.) If I didn't know better, I'd take him to be saying, "Great walk, Boss!"

Would I take the morning walk, religiously, day after day and year after year, if Jacques weren't with me? Doubtful. All my life I've prided myself in never keeping up any kind of regular exercise program.

The walk does us good. When I got Jacques from the shelter, a grown dog, three or four years old, he weighed fifty-nine pounds and was jumpy, nervous, and scrawny. Apparently the daily walk is all it has taken to make him into the massive, friendly, alert, and dignified athlete he is today. That and regular meals, such medical care as he has required, and, of course, the relationship.

In the more than a thousand times I've taken that walk, I've never been bored for a moment. I might get bored, but Jacques is incapable of it and his enthusiasm rubs off on me.

Jacques is not the first dog I've lived with, and doubtless won't be the last. The choice to live with dogs—which amounts, in my case, to a necessity—is something a non-dog-owning individual finds hard to understand. And people who like to live with dogs, especially those who write about them, never tire of explaining the attraction.

The standard explanation is this: "Because dogs give us humans uncritical, uncompromising, unconditional love." That's what all the TV documentaries say. That's what most books and articles say too.

What's so good about uncritical, uncompromising, unconditional love? Speaking for myself, if anyone, or anything, loves me, I'm only going to feel good about it if I'm loved for my qualities—or, anyway, a quality.

I'm not arguing that dogs do not love their humans without reservation. I'm just questioning whether that, all by itself, is a reason to want to live with one. Dogs are stupid compared to us. It's easy to fool them. As silly and vain as humans are, I can't believe that the whole big deal between us and dogs is because they are foolish enough to look up to us.

Most dogs are terribly informal creatures. They do things in company that we would only do in private. In fact, they do things in company that we would not do, even in private—this is true of me, anyway, and I hope of the reader.

Dogs tend to study us, but they make no conclusions. They observe us, but they do not judge us. I submit that under this kind of benign scrutiny we begin to feel comfortable about observing ourselves. It isn't possible to have self-knowledge when completely alone, and it is difficult except in unusual and specific circumstances to be absolutely ourselves when in another's company.

It is not the mere fact of Jacques's generous affection that makes him important to me. It is that through a connection with him I begin to know, and maybe even accept, myself.

Is that a reason to live with a creature, care for it, accommodate it, study it, try to understand it, and love it?

I think so. I think it's an excellent reason. So far in my life I've had only a few friends as satisfactory as Jacques—and half of those friends have been dogs.

THE PUG
Dan Yaccarino

Pugs are my favorite kind of dog. Whenever I'm walking around my neighborhood and I see one, I must pet it. What with that little wet nose, pushed-in face, and worried look, who can resist?

The Eyes Have It

Arthur Yorinks

I'm one of the lucky ones. I grew up with dogs. My father, a stubborn man with a heart of gold, loves animals. He's the sort who picked up box turtles abandoned unceremoniously on the Belt Parkway, in Brooklyn, and brought them home and had my brother and me hand-feed them hamburger every day. He's the sort that in the seventeen years I'd lived with him he brought home at least a dog a year, probably more. His affection for canines has no discernible limits.

One day, when I was five, my father went to the foot doctor to have a corn removed, and he came home with a Bouvier des Flandres. There he stood, in the basement, next to a pony (that's what I thought it was) and whispered to me, "The doctor couldn't keep him anymore. Don't tell your mother."

So I love dogs. I've lived with beagles and poodles and sheepdogs and Labradors and wolfhounds and spaniels and mutts of every concoction. And now, in midlife, I have a confession to make. I have developed a dog preference. No, it doesn't matter to me whether they are tall or short, furry or silky, fat or skinny. What matters to me is whether or not they have gorilla eyeballs. Perhaps not a scientific term yet, gorilla eyeballs is a specific canine trait discovered by me when I was seven years old.

At that time I lived with a fairly enormous standard poodle, and she had eyes that reminded me of a gorilla. Not that my father ever brought home a gorilla. I simply concluded that these large brown eyes with lots of white around them contained the wisdom of the ages, or at least the wisdom of gorillas. When I spoke to her, I knew she understood me. And I also knew she could respond to me if she wanted to, but simply chose not to. "You know what I'm thinking," she said with her eyes.

Some dogs use their tails to let us know what's on their minds. Some wave their bulky bodies around and whip themselves into an elaborate dance: "I want to go out!"

"I want something to eat!" "Pet me, scratch me, rub my ears now!" Dogs go in for exclamation points.

Some dogs like to use their legs and feet. Depending on proximity, they scratch the air or your leg or wooden furniture that must be refinished at great expense. "Hey, you," with a scratch. "I'm talking to you," another few scratches, "and I'm hungry, so go to the pantry and put some food in my bowl—now!" Dogs don't trouble themselves with minutes or hours. Time is either "now!" or "right now!"

Well, after years of living with body-waving, barking, and paw-scratching canines, I've devoted my life to gorilla-eyeball dogs. I live with five Border collies and one red poodle. All eyes. Indeed, in some circles, the Border collie is called the eye dog. Their eyes, like a carpenter's hammer, are their tools of the trade. They use them, like a preacher's sermon, to show their flock the way.

Sometimes, when I think about it, it seems that dogs have a bad deal. We teach them to sit and stay and roll over. They teach us dignity and heroism and the unfettered joy in being yourself. Have you ever seen a golden retriever mope around wishing she was a spitz?

Dogs have saved my life. And here is a story of just the beginning of my debt being repaid. It's a true story.

*

There was a hurricane coming. The CBC Radio had predicted it for the last several days, and now that it had side-swiped Boston it seemed to be on course for Cape Breton, Nova Scotia.

I was in my studio, looking out at the ocean and thinking, This must be the calm before the storm. There was a stunning blue-green color to the sea and the sky was a placid, overcast gray. The water was still. Like a lake.

Adrienne, my wife, was putting a leash on Ruggles. Out of the four Border collies we had then, Ruggles was the only one that needed a leash to go for a walk. He was blind and somewhat mentally imbalanced. Not a euphemism. He suffered from a rare brain disease that would take his life before the age of two. But now, this summer, he still had months to live, to be loved, to be cared for by us, to give us his boundless love.

Before the thousand-mile trip to our home in Canada, I had our friend and neighbor put up a fence and create a kind of backyard. It looked ridiculous in that our house sits alone on a cliff that extends for a couple of miles in each direction. The ocean resides a few hundred feet in front of us, at the bottom of a seventy-foot drop from the verdant emerald coastline. Behind us one can see the small mountains of Cape Breton.

This unspoiled landscape was made for a Border collie. Originated on the border of England and Scotland, Border collies would find this "new Scotland" of Canada heaven. Ours did. Rounding up birds and running to their hearts content was pure joy. Discounting the lack of sheep, the dogs were having a perfect vacation. Bongo, as she has done since her first trip to Nova Scotia, sat in the grass and sniffed the air. In the morning she gazed east, to the mountains. In the afternoon, she looked west, to the ocean. Selma and her daughter Ida waited for someone to throw tennis balls into the juniper, the farther the better. And Ruggles. Ruggles just waited. He wanted to do something. For all of his screwed up and diseased genes he was still a Border collie. Adrienne knew this. She decided to try to take him, along with the others, for a walk along the coast.

We had packed an extra-long leash, the one we learned to use so Ruggles could have some freedom without hurting himself. I watched my animal family from my window as they made their way along the hay-field path to the cliff—a mixture of reindeer moss, juniper, and cranberry patches. If a wealthy man tried to have the most magnificent carpeting made, he could not match this weave.

Cradling the telephone, I remarked to a friend how gorgeous the landscape was, just as I saw the heads of the three healthy dogs bolt up. A scent, probably deer, ignited canine noses. They looked to the left, toward the woods, and ran. Ruggles, sensing movement, maybe registering the scent, certainly wanting to join his pack, ran too. He ran with such force that he knocked Adrienne to the ground and in doing so tore the leash from her hand. Suddenly, this pastoral scene turned into a wrenching nightmare. Adrienne sprang to her feet and turned to Ruggles, who was between her and the edge of the cliff and the ocean. She called to him in a firm, but controlled voice. "Ruggles—come. Ruggles—come!" He cocked his ear; he moved backward; he turned. "Ruggles! RUGGLES!" Adrienne was screaming. Ruggles whipped around and ran. He ran off the cliff.

Adrienne yelled out his name once more as I slammed the phone down and ran out of the house. As I ran toward her, Adrienne was screaming and crying and running toward the large juniper near Sadie's cranberry patch. Tied around the juniper was a rope our neighbors, when they were kids, thirty or forty years ago, used to climb down to the rocks and the sea. Before I could reach her, Adrienne grabbed the rope, which immediately disin-tegrated in her hands. She started to try to climb down the cliff as I caught up with her.

"Wait, let me get the other dogs in," I said as I tried to calm her down. She cried and I held her and told her to wait so that we could find a safe place to climb down. The three dogs, hearing Adrienne's voice, had already come back from the woods, and I called to them to follow me. I ran back to the house with the dogs behind me and I tried to get the images, the horrible images of Ruggles on the rocks, out of my head. There are no veterinarians within fifty miles at least, so what would we do? Far removed from the life of emergency rooms and friendly doctors, I wondered if Germie, one of our closer neighbors, had a gun.

"Go in," I instructed, and the dogs reluctantly went into the house. I shut the door and ran back to the edge of the cliff, where Adrienne had already started climbing down. There are only one or two spots along the mile-long coast to get down to the rocks; the face of the cliff is mostly shale and sandstone. I followed Adrienne down, and she asked me what I already had thought of—did I think Germie had a gun.

When we reached the rocks and the water, we headed as quickly as we could to where Ruggles had leaped. We both spotted him at the same time. He was standing, almost motionless, on a rock. Standing! Stunned, relieved, surprised, thanking God, and in a release of emotion, laughing, we approached Ruggles and called his name. He heard us and wagged his tail. I went over to him and found nothing out of the ordinary except for a slight scratch on his snout. Surely he is bleeding internally, I thought. His bones must be broken. What are we going to do?

"We have to get him up the cliff," Adrienne said, and for a brief moment we both entertained the idea that somehow we could carry him up the cliff. The brief moment passed. It was almost impossible for us to get down without killing ourselves. But maybe an alternative would be to carry him along the rocks to a beach about a mile south as the crow flies. Probably two or three miles, in the twists and turns of the coastline.

As I moved to try to pick Ruggles up, all seventy pounds of him, I realized I'd never be able to do it. The rocks, nicely polished by the relentless ocean, were slippery, and I had an instant vision of falling and both of us, dog and man, breaking our necks.

We sat there, Adrienne and I, in the calm of having our Ruggles alive, in the calm of the still ocean, and thought. A boat, some kind of boat, seemed like the only answer. But the only person we knew who had a boat lived almost fifteen miles away. The hurricane was coming. We could sense it. The wind was picking up, and the air became thick with moisture.

"What about that rubber thing you bought last year?" Adrienne asked. In a Melvillian fantasy of sailing, I had purchased a cheap rubber boat in Caldor for $39.95. According to the box, which I never opened, it held three adults and came with two air chambers (as a safety), its own pump, and a couple of oars. It sat in our storage room, untouched.

In the vacuum of other ideas, this seemed like a stroke of brilliance. I sprang up and headed along the rocks, back to the spot where one could, with difficulty, climb up the cliff. Slipping and falling four times into the water along the

way convinced me that carrying Ruggles was never a good idea. And now, as I struggled against the shale, gripping for what seemed like my life, even the boating idea lost some of its charm.

I ran to our house, my dungarees heavy with ocean water, my Reeboks squishing and sloshing, and opened the door. In what seemed like ten seconds I tore open the boat box, grabbed the folded rubber boat, a couple of oars, and oh, no, the plastic step-on-it-with-your-foot pump. I ran out of the house again to the "safe spot" along the cliff. I threw what I had in my hands down to the rocks and slid, not on purpose, down myself.

Grabbing the paraphernalia, I returned to Adrienne and Ruggles. He was sitting now on the same rock and Adrienne was singing to him. When she saw me she burst out laughing. "It'll just be a couple of hours, hon, and your cruise will be departing," I said.

I hooked up the pump and began to inflate the Caldor special. In my prophesied time frame, the boat was seaworthy. We cast it out, holding onto the rope that circumvented the outside, and Adrienne tried to steady it. I took hold of Ruggles, who began to bite my hand out of fear, and I lowered him into the boat. For a minute this scene, this postcard picture, endured. There was Ruggles, sitting in a boat in the ocean, wind blowing his magnificent black-and-white coat. There was something funny and pathetic and joyful and sad all at once. I thought of Roman Polanski's *Three Men and a Wardrobe,* except we were two people and a blind Border collie.

Adrienne got into the boat next and, after some negotiating, got Ruggles to lie down. She stroked him and tried to calm him as I took hold of the rope.

This would be simple. I'd pull the boat and its contents along the shore until we reached the beach. Then I'd race back along the highway and get our car and come back and pick them up.

I took one step and found myself immersed in water up to my nose. The idea that I could, like some grand work-horse, pull this boat along the coast without slipping was moronic. I'll have to swim, I thought.

And so I did. For about three miles, with the rope in one hand, I swam—as close to the shore as I could—as if I were Superman. I don't know how I did it. My heart felt as if it were going to burst.

The clouds grew darker. Adrienne panicked when the boat began to sway in the waves. If it tipped over, Ruggles might drown. And racing through my dark mind was the possibility of us all drowning. There was no turning back now. I was as far from our launching point as I was from my destination. It began to drizzle. If the hurricane hits now, if I got a cramp, if I let go of the boat, if a wave capsizes the boat—these were my thoughts.

I tried to think about summer camp. The few saving graces of my childhood camp experience were that I learned to swim and that my parents loved the two royal standard poodles that lived with the camp owner. The next summer, when I was seven, they drove to Kingston, New York, and bought a poodle. She and I swam in Lake Champlain, and I remembered how cold it was.

But, thanks to the Gulf Stream, which bends around the northern tip of Cape Breton and hugs the coast, this ocean water was warm. So I swam and swam, hoping each bend or curve was the promised land, the beach at Terre Noire. After an hour and a half, maybe two, I spotted land. The driftwood-strewn beach never looked so good.

I pulled the boat up onto the rocky sand and Adrienne got out first. We lifted Ruggles from the boat, and to our amazement he stood there, shaken but practically unfazed. Surely something had to be wrong; surely some bones must be broken.

I ran up the pathway to the Cabot Trail and ran alongside for another mile and a half to the road that leads to our house. The rain was coming down more steadily now. I got in the car and drove back to the beach. Adrienne had already walked, with Ruggles, up the path. Both jumped into the car.

The wind was picking up as I pulled down our road. We walked into the house as the hurricane hit. They clocked the winds at eighty miles an hour. Ruggles ate his home-cooked hamburger-mixed-with-kibble dinner with an equal fury. He was unharmed.

At the end of that summer my mother asked me, How did Ruggles do up in Canada? Without going into it, I told her he had a great time. He went skydiving. He went swimming. He went boating.

I have found that, when it comes to dogs, even true stories are miracles.

MOONDOG AND BOUTROS BOUTROS-GHALI
Karen Barbour

My dogs bark too much. They dig under the fence and chase the neighbor's cat. They dig big channels in the garden, trying to catch gophers. At night they run off; I hear Moondog howling. When they come back, panting with wild eyes, they smell like skunks and run through the house trying to rub the scent on the couches. The dogs sleep in our bed and wake us up in the middle of the night with their scratching. They have been to dog-training classes twice and graduated with honors. We also had a private trainer come for eight weeks and they minded perfectly until she left.

We found Moondog at the pound. He was so skinny his ribs poked out, and he lay on the concrete floor with his front paws crossed. I fell in love with him. I put my face close to the bars and he put his head back and howled. His fur was oily; I could smell him from far away. He was a long-legged, filthy hound dog that had been living in a van with two other dogs and a family of five. He had never been in a house before. They said he killed cats.

I left the Humane Society but couldn't stop thinking about him. I kept calling to see if he was still there.

When I dragged my husband down to see him, he was appalled. He did not want that dog; he wanted a puppy. We went to dog shelters, dark barracks with sad old dogs curled up and crazy, exuberant young dogs and mean-looking ones.

We went up to Napa County to look at some coonhounds. The man had about fifteen dogs in a pen: black-and-tan coonhounds and treeing walker coonhounds like Moondog. The only puppy that was left had been bitten and his face was swollen. He looked terrible. The man used his dogs to hunt bear.

We went further north and met a woman who bred chocolate Labs. The females were short and squat, and there was one big male who looked at us with yellow eyes. I felt like leaving as soon as we got there. In the backyard, eleven puppies crawled over one another. Our son picked one up and I knew we would be taking it home.

We drove to the pound and introduced the puppy to Moondog. We had both dogs in a fenced-in area and Moondog sniffed the puppy all over. Moondog went to the corner and lifted his leg.

Our baby climbs on the dogs and lies on them and pulls their ears and feeds them his dinner. He chews on their toys and they chew on his. Boutros always lies in the shade and Moondog lies in the sun. They always remind me at exactly 6:00 P.M. that they want their dinner, and they sing if anyone plays the harmonica.

KAREN BARBOUR

KAREN BARBOUR

KAREN BARBOUR

KAREN BARBOUR

KAREN BARBOUR

Mr. and Mrs. Foo

Enid Shomer

Among my family treasures is a cracked black-and-white photograph of my grandmother Minerva at the wheel of her white 1949 Ford convertible, her face partly eclipsed by a stylish felt hat, her dark eyes peering across the years to meet mine. In the passenger seat, grinning sheepishly, is Grandfather Aleck, a silent, absentminded "character" (my grandmother's term) who left cigarettes burning in every room. In the palmy background, Miami inches sweatily toward air-conditioning and land booms. On the backseat of the car, in all their furry ferocity and elegance, sit as if enthroned a matched set of Chow Chows: Mr. and Mrs. Foo.

I knew these dogs only from a distance. They were said not to like the unpredictable, sudden movements of children. In fact, they disdained everyone but my grand-parents and each other. Not even adults dared challenge those scowling eyes, the rumble in their throats, the ears flicking forward and back with telegraphic if not telepathic import. The year I lived in Florida as a child and in subsequent summer visits, Mr. and Mrs. Foo always remained six inches beyond my reach, a space defined on one side by my hand trembling with all the yearning a child has for another living thing, on the other by their apprehensive faces. I do not think I ever managed to pet either one of them.

Their intolerant temperaments may have had as much to do with the climate as their breeding. They groused con-tinually in their small corner of my grandmother's apart-ment, behind her beauty parlor. On the wall above them, an oscillating fan whipped up a sticky wind that closed their eyes precisely, like dolls, once each sweep, and buttoned and unbuttoned their thick coats. Tufts of russet fur floated and collected everywhere. Perhaps because Grandmother spent her days with her hands in other people's hair, she did not mind continual shedding. I remember the floor of her shop as an unrelenting alphabet of wet C's—hair clippings of every color.

Much can be gleaned about my grandmother from this photo: the philosophy of living rich and dying poor—which often backfired on her—her love of dogs, and her hunger for drama and glamour on a grand scale. She chauffeured them about with the top down, as if they were a pair of giant fashion accessories.

Despite their crabby temperaments—or perhaps because of them—Mr. and Mrs. Foo, the first canines in our family, converted us to dog lovers. They made dog owning seem a great privilege, an extravagance rather than a practicality. These dogs toiled not, neither did they spin or herd sheep. Nor did my grandmother come from a dog-owning tradition that would have required them to be useful as opposed to merely decorative. In her native Romania, a dog in the Jewish shtetl was a superfluity not worth feeding, a dirty walking insult to the concept of kosher. I believe she owned dogs (and the Ford) to cast off the constraints of the Old World and bathe in the ethos of a country that considered dogs wholesome family additions, ambassadors of wisdom from whom one could learn invaluable lessons about love and death. "A parakeet is nice, like a feather on a hat," she always said (she kept two), "but a dog is a *mensch*."

Bought, no doubt, in the same spirit of down-home orientalism as bathroom wallpaper with repeating bamboo footbridges, Mr. and Mrs. Foo nevertheless gave me a taste for the beautiful. The notion of having any aesthetic at all begins in the backseat of that convertible with those two hopelessly ill-suited imperial hunters of China panting through the torrid Augusts of south Florida. With those unnaturally black gums and blue-black tongues begins my appreciation for the unusual, for the thing brought into existence by vision, the wrought object, the ideal of perfection that propels my writing and love of all the arts. (Here I include the years I spent breeding dogs, from which I learned proportion, balance, and, most importantly, judgment—how to *see:* a painting, an Arabian horse, a dog, with a passionately dispassionate, critical eye.)

Intended as watchdogs, Mr. and Mrs. Foo ended up being the things we watched, icons of all that lay beyond the hardscrabble struggle for survival that was my grandmother's life and her mother's life before her. I would go so far as to say that in her slant-ceilinged, two-bedroom flat with leaky jalousies and buckling linoleum, they stood for culture, or at least the pretension of culture, which is very nearly the same thing. And we loved them, out of respect for their Chow Chow-ness, for all that set them exotically apart. Even today, reduced to an image only two inches high, dead nearly forty years, they move me to awe. I can still remember how utterly breathtaking they were, walking in tandem, alerting nobly to the same sounds. They were my first encounter with the beautiful uselessness that feeds the soul, the nonstop obstinacies that lie at the heart of love and of art.

Take That, Will Rogers

Steven Bauer

I never met a dog I didn't like.

When I was growing up, I heard this said not about dogs but about people, a sentiment I found deeply mystifying, even stupid. As far as I was able to tell, this Mr. Rogers, who had first admitted liking all people, was grown up, had the benefit of years of experience, and still had not discovered what I already knew at a very young age. I had found that there were lots of people I didn't like, lots of people who weren't worth liking. The neighborhood bully, for example, who had tied me to a tree and made me smoke a whole pack of Winstons; Miss Searle, my teacher, who was a fanatic about the flutophone; our next-door neighbors, the Mienkes, whose devotion to their lawn precluded my ever

traversing it. Though I was young, I'd learned that people could be mean and petty, blustery, braggadocious, exclusionary, obtuse, selfish, and cruel. At the time—don't ask me how this is possible—I knew no dogs, and so the concept of peace, goodwill, and charity toward an entire species was alien to me. But it is no longer.

Sure, I've run into several dogs I was wary of, and one or two whose personal habits have put me off—incessant and annoying barking, or an obsession with the human knee—but by and large my major impulse, when I see a dog, is to stop whatever I'm doing and say hello. I hesitate to write about this because it makes me seem like the sort of sentimentalist who goes all weepy at the sight of painted puppies and kitties with eyes the size of dinner plates, and this is emphatically not the case. I don't feel all weak and fuzzy inside when I see a dog; I feel, rather, exhilarated and interested, braced, ready for the world to take on new colorations and possibilities. Dogs, with their nose-to-the-ground, tail-wagging eagerness, their let-me-at-that-squirrel enthusiasm, remind me that what might on some days seem routine or dreary is only that way if you refuse to see the world at each moment with new eyes.

I couldn't tell you how many times our small pack has made its way across the fenced acre we have for them — enough times, anyway, for them to know each blade of grass intimately. And yet every morning when they charge out the back door and into the field, it's with the wide-eyed amazement of Cortez on a peak in Darien. What new wonder waits in store? What new outrage? Which other animals have left their scents and scat? Have the farmers momentarily deserted a piece of bizarre-looking and totally terrifying machinery the pack wants to flee from but will nevertheless bark at bravely as it stands its ground? Are the cows standing moon-faced and foreign, great impressionist splotches of black and white begging to be harried? What new rodents can be unearthed? What new cats scared up a tree?

Sure, I love our dogs, all five of them. But I'm not overly discriminating. I'll stop to schmooze with any dog I meet. I'll be walking down the sidewalk and happen upon a Labrador tied to a parking meter, her human having momentarily ducked into a storefront, and I can no more pass without saying hello than some people can pass a baby carriage without peeking inside. The

Lab will be lying patiently, her red lead a smart contrast to her shiny black coat, and I'll hunker down and start talking. To their credit, not every dog is wild about this sort of attention from a stranger, but almost every one has the dignity to let me say a few words and even the forbearance to receive a pat.

When I'm driving, I notice dogs taking their humans for a walk, and I sometimes almost go off the road as I follow their trajectory. At such moments, I'm always cheered by something I notice — the particular feathered arc of a setter's tail as she wags, or the vertiginous tripodic balance of a hound outdoing himself by lifting his leg higher than it's ever been lifted before, the ear-flapping hell-bent-for-leather leaping of a water spaniel after a Frisbee, or the elbows-into-it digging of a beagle, intent on something he thinks he hears underground. Such heartfelt animation, such total interest in life! O brave new world, that has such creatures in't.

It was not always so, for I grew up without dogs. How I managed this, I'm not sure, but I wouldn't recommend it, and I wouldn't try it again. Surrounded as I currently am, this is utterly strange to me now, so foreign, so unlikely, that it seems the childhood of someone else.

My grandmother, who lived with us, was allergic to dog dander, or so the story went. She was an odd woman who paid me to pick the Japanese beetles from her roses and to gather fallen crabapples from the neighbor's yard for jelly. She lived in the attic room upstairs, sipped tea, and listened on Saturday afternoons to Milton Cross broadcast the Metropolitan Opera. From her I got my love of books and reading, which is an enormous debt I owe her. Yet at the same time, if my parents can be trusted, she deprived me of a dog.

I had some small pet turtles once, bought at Woolworth's; they had greenish shells about the size of a half-dollar, made up of concentric overlapping squares. They lived in a plastic oval with a circular ramp at the top of which a vivid plastic palm tree waved its fronds. I was interested in the turtles, but not overly fond of them. Still, I tried to imagine what it was like to *be* a turtle, and one chill October morning, when they were particularly frisky after a night spent outside on the back patio, I imagined they must be very cold indeed, and so I emptied their oval home and filled it with nice warm water. My grief was intense but short-lived, and more about guilt than love. For a time I had gold-fish, brought home in a no-frills plastic bag filled with water and later flushed down the toilet. I caught lightning bugs and kept them in a jar.

But no dogs. No dogs anywhere in my early memories. None of my friends had dogs, and the neighbors with their immaculate lawn certainly didn't have dogs. I can't conjure up pictures of impatient suit-jacketed men dragging dogs around the neighborhood for their morning constitutionals, and there were no dogs that ran loose, joining our pack of boys. The only dogs that come to mind when I scan those years were kept in winter inside the padlocked fortress known as the Spring Lake Country Club, whose sylvan name gives no indication of shepherds hurling themselves against the chain-links, snarling.

This enclave was several miles from where I lived, and an entirely different world. To get there, my buddies and I had first to cross a stretch of woods, then an honest-to-God swamp with hillocks of swamp grass on which we stood as we readied ourselves for the jump to the next one, then several fields, until we came to the moonscape which was the slag and detritus from the construction of the country club itself. The heaps of slag were immense and good for running up and down, but inevitably we'd pass beyond this outsize playground and be face to face with the chain-link fence.

None of us belonged to the country club; none of us had ever even been inside, and so, of course, now that it was closed up tight for the winter, we climbed. There were three of us, and all three had gotten over the fence and had started to explore when we heard the barking. It came from the distance and grew precipitously louder, and we decided without much consultation that it might be a good idea to get back over the fence, just as the dogs burst into view. This aided our climbing ability, and we were safely on the other side of the fence by the time the shepherds became airborne. I remember standing there and staring at those magnificent full-chested beasts, amazed at the raspberry color of their tongues and their gleaming teeth. Yes, I was frightened, but I wasn't traumatized. Somehow even then, I knew that these dogs, given another chance, would be happy to lick my hand. They'd been taught to act that way; they were, in fact, no longer dogs at all, but projections of the rage and fear some people use dogs to embody. I understood even then that dogs don't bite people—people bite people.

*

I read *Lassie Come Home* one summer, lying on the porch glider while outside; the tar on the pavement softened and bubbled and the sound of lawnmowers intermittently disturbed the quiet. That was the same summer I went to day camp and learned the box stitch so that I could make clunky, ugly, and uncomfortable plastic bracelets for my mom and lanyards for my dad, so I could play kickball in the dust. But mostly I remember lying on that glider as it rocked back and forth, my bare, sweaty back sticking to the heavy vinyl as tears sheeted down my cheeks.

I had never felt such grief before, grief, of course, that was alleviated by the time I reached the end of the book; nevertheless, what I felt seemed to me purer, more powerful, more sincere than most of the feelings I'd ever had. That was one of the times I went to my parents and asked for a dog. But I was told then, as I was told every other time I asked, that my grandmother would sneeze her way to heaven if we had a dog, and so there were no ifs, ands, or buts about it: the answer was no. After a while, I gave up. I was consigned to a dogless life. I can't help but think that many of the peculiar sadnesses of my boyhood, which even now won't dissipate, which roll around inside me like a handful of marbles, might well have been lightened or erased by a dog.

Now there are five. Though this sometimes seems like too many—when they're all in the same room and desirous of attention—it can also seem like just the right number, since they are clearly so different, one from the other, in size and color, in quirks and foibles, in personalities. There's Minimum, who lies buried each morning under a quilt in a large willow basket, in a nook by the bedroom window, and if she hasn't already roused herself by the time I'm up I unearth her, our little Lazarus. I lift the quilt

and there she is, sober and waiting, on her back, curved like the half-moon outside the window, her four legs in the air, her four paws a friend of ours has compared to fuzzy bedroom slippers dangling. I pick her up, and we head downstairs. On the way, she'll be looking at me serenely or fixedly, depending on the dream she'd been having, and she might even experiment, a furtive lick to the cheek, to make sure the tongue's working this morning.

There's Pippin, the newest member of our pack, about the same size as Minnie, but otherwise as dissimilar to her as a dog can be. Pip's a controlled nuclear explosion, a chewer and a digger. She was put on earth to play, not to think, as Minnie was. Pippin is part beagle, and so fast when she's on a tear that truly one's eyes can barely keep up with her. Our fence will not contain her, and she spends hours each day plotting her escape, so that she can make it over to the neighbors' farm, where there are cows and geese to chase and where all manner of sweet and rotting thing can be found to roll in, ecstatically, as though the very best aspect of being a dog is carrying the smells back home.

Under the counter, in the nook we thought might house a chair or stool, lurks Gabrielle. She's as unlikely a dog as I've ever seen—part basset, part German shepherd. Her legs are short and stubby, and her ears are velvety and enormous, but her head and coloring are classic shepherd. She's more like an elephant seal than a dog, really, hungry for human companionship, though a bit of a coward. Her essential personality was clear from the start: Trust no one, and run from danger. When we enter the kitchen she looks up apprehensively to make sure it's really us; once, when she mistook my wife for an intruder, she slunk around the corner without making a sound and made herself as small as possible—not an easy task.

Chance is part terrier and a dog with a mission—he believes he was put on earth to guard our property. We have not taught him to do this; he merely believes his place is on the front porch, paws hanging over the top step, as he lies and watches, alert to every nuance of the landscape, every movement in the distance—cow, hawk, dog. Whatever it is, he barks at it, to let us know there's danger in the offing. I sometimes think he must be exhausted from carrying all that responsibility, and he is—surely—for whenever we let him in, he almost immediately falls asleep.

I come last to the alpha dog of our pack, Pittsburgh, a gorgeous tawny hound with soul-filled kohl-rimmed eyes and an inexhaustibly curious and hopeful nature. At 100 pounds, he can look formidable to a stranger, I imagine, but he has the nature of a puppy. He still likes to sit in our laps, as he did when he was little. He was born upstairs, under the bed in the front bedroom, on a cold January night almost eleven years ago, and knowing him has changed my life forever. For years he has tried to master English and has come quite close on several occasions. He is as gracious as he is large, as tolerant of foolishness among the younger members of the pack as the perfect father would be. He has as much spirit, as much goodness in him as could be found in an average-size American town and, when he wants to love you, an absolutely frontal assault that can leave you actually breathless.

When all five dogs are together in a room, the resulting tumult, the conflicting desires, the vocalizations, can get a bit daunting. Minnie will want a bit of solitude, while Gabrielle will believe that not heard is not seen; Pippin will be inflicting upon Gabrielle her insatiable interest, while Chance might well raise his muzzle and croon. And over it all, Pittsburgh will canter, regal and a bit anxious, hoping for a chewie. It's at moments like this that I catch myself, fierce believer in regulating the number of one's offspring as I am, understanding those parents who find themselves having just one more child, and then one beyond that. I remind myself that I didn't have these dogs, that all but one of them came because someone else abandoned them. Sure, the costs and difficulties multiply, but so does the joy.

I know I am preaching to the converted here, but nevertheless. . . . I still believe that I was right as a child to distrust Will Rogers's naive faith in humankind, and I still believe that my current parallel faith in dogs is not misfounded. Much has been written about the loyalty of dogs, but what I love about them isn't their devotion to me so much as their devotion to being alive. I love their open-hearted willingness to take the world on its own terms. Let me at it, they say; sock it to me. Here I come, ready or not. Let the games begin.

EARLY DOG
James Balog

I took these photos of the Basenji and the Labrador retriever in a pitch-black room. While the camera's shutter was open, I used a high-tech, fiber optic flashlight to "paint" light down the animal. What I hadn't expected was a rather surreal experience.

One moment revealed a glimpse of the dog, the next moment obscured it again. This appearing and disappearing suddenly presented me with an image of early man, sitting in a cave and sighting, in the flickering of the firelight, the fleeting image of the first dog.

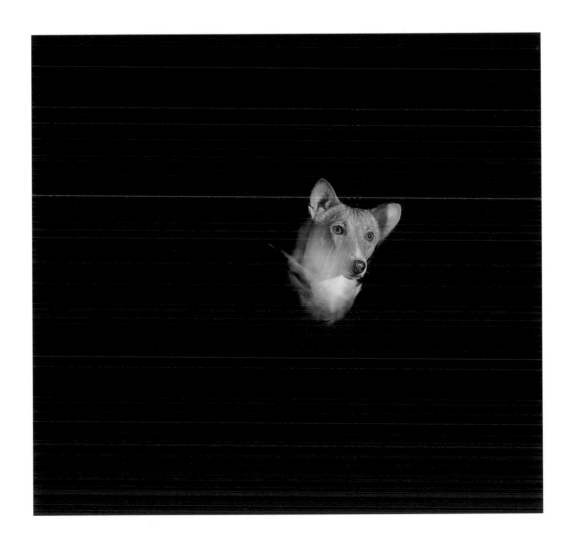

JAMES BALOG

Newshounds

Steve Rushin

As any newshound will tell you, dogs and newspapers share a glorious history. Dogs are the very definition of a great news story ("Man Bites Dog"). The earliest available edition of an American newspaper is called the bulldog edition. A dog is trained to go on the paper, or to fetch a rolled-up paper for its master. All of this may help explain why dogs were my only companions at four o'clock on summer mornings as I delivered the bulldog edition of the *Minneapolis Tribune*. Every day without fail, a canine cast of characters awaited my predawn arrival with bated dog breath.

Dogs can't shake, like bathwater, their reputation for menacing mailmen, those scary uniformed soldiers packing Mace—a kind of Spot-remover, if you will. But I can attest that dogs love paperboys bearing Marmaduke and Snoopy and all the news from Dogpatch. The squeaking steel wheels of the cart required to caddy the fat Sunday editions were pri-

vate music to the floppy ears of the dogs on my route, dogs who dogged me up and down the streets, falling in line behind the Pied Paperboy of Bloomington, Minnesota.

As the suburbs slept, I led a canine conga line across tidy lawns damp with dew, scattering rolled-up papers like dry bones to doorsteps. In the shafts of light thrown by street lamps, we were shown in sharp relief: Me and the Dalmatian whose old-lady owner dressed him in a scarlet cardigan at Christmas, giving new life to the old newspaper riddle "What's black and white and red all over?" Or me and the doctor's dog, who would be turned out on rare occasions in a physician's smock. *A black Lab in a white lab coat.* Even at twelve, I had to wonder about these people who would turn their pets into puns.

In fact, my route was dog-collar-studded with residents who anthropomorphized their mutts. Viewed from above, the circular subdevelopment, covered in grass like green baize, must have looked like a live-action version of that famous painting masterwork *Dogs Playing Poker,* though I don't recall any basset hounds in green eyeshades. If there had been such a dog, this adolescent aspiring reporter would have imagined the pooch as a '40s-vintage newspaper editor, barking those vaguely dog-related orders that editors like to bark: *Get the poop . . . What's the scoop? . . .*

I like to think that dogs are the most literate of animals. What's black and white and read by Rover? It must be the newspaper, for there were many houses in which the *people* couldn't possibly have ordered the subscription. These were the houses with Beware of Dog signs, which usually meant Beware of Owner. He was invariably some nut-job from whom it would be impossible to collect payment at the end of the summer. Ring the doorbell. I hear the scratch of nails on hallway linoleum. And . . . nobody answers. The dog is eager to greet his paperboy, but the homeowner is playing dead.

Alas, when I finally became a reporter myself I knew the dogs on my old route were not awaiting my copy, for it was published in magazines, which are delivered—alas, alas— by mailmen. And what's worse, on one of my earliest assignments for *Sports Illustrated,* I learned that profane newspapermen are not always Dog's Best Friend.

In researching the worst baseball team of all time, the 1962 New York Mets, I discovered that the team had a mascot named Homer the Beagle and he lived at the Waldorf-Astoria, on Park Avenue in Manhattan. Oh, what a wonderful time that was to be young and single and a beagle living in Gotham! And if you happened to be a big-

league baseball mascot on top of that, well, then the world was indeed your Gaines-Burger.

Homer (I like to think he was named for the Greek poet) was trained by Rudd Weatherwax, the man who taught Lassie everything he knew. Unfortunately, the Weatherwaxian magic did not work on Homer, who never got the hang of circling the bases at the Polo Grounds. Of course, neither did the Mets that year, but it was Homer who was humiliated in the rabid New York tabloid press. The beagle was said to have spent his exile brooding over his bad notices, holed up in his suite at the Waldorf, surrounded by magnificent baubles but miserable inside. Both despondent and ridiculous, Homer had come to resemble that most famous of newspaper magnates. He was Charles Foster Kanine.

Of course, Homer is long gone, and newspapers are disappearing, as well. Like the rest of us, dogs are turning away from the print media, and those days when a hound heard "Pound" and thought "Ezra" are becoming but a memory. Today's dogs would rather listen to a CD— factory-sealed with little foil stickers called "dog-bones" in the music industry—by some doggerel rapper like Snoop Doggy Dogg. Or watch TV, torn between the euphony of Bob Barker's name and the game-show host's ominous have-your-pet-spayed-or-neutered message at the end of his program.

Still, I like to think there is a new litter of literati out there somewhere, that dogs are still the most literate of animals. And that the descendants of those dogs on my old paper route might even pause and slobber over this essay, and remember their forbears fondly.

And perhaps even dog-ear the page.

Mason the Dream Girl

Cynthia Heimel

My friend Patti always talked about her dog, Mason. Mason blah blah blah, Mason went to the beach, Mason blah, Mason has tapeworms, Mason doesn't have tapeworms, blah blah, Mason got her shots, blah.

Naturally I fell in love with Mason sight unseen, especially since Patti's face took on this Mason-glow as she talked. I invited myself to dinner to meet this fab canine.

Patti was fooling around in her wheelchair, wild-eyed and worried that she'd screw up dinner. It was a small apartment, no dog in sight.

"Where's Mason?"

"In the bedroom. She's mad at me because I gave her a bath. She'll come out eventually."

We ate appetizers. No Mason. We started dinner. No Mason. Was she Patti's imaginary friend? Every dog comes to visit during dinner. I put my fork down.

"Let's go see Mason, I can't stand it another second," I said.

We went into the bedroom. There she was. Lying on a folded-up quilt next to the bed, glaring reproachfully. A small-ish red dog, retriever-spaniel face, hair fluffed out. Her muzzle was white; her back was curved with arthritis. Her eyes were cloudy, but not too cloudy to be tender and stoic. A fragile, elderly girl.

"Hello Mason, you old bag," I sang in my screechy, stupid doggy voice.

"She can't hear you. She's deaf as a post."

Mason stood up creakily and walked over to me, looked me in the eye, yawned a big cloud of unbelievably pungent doggy-breath, and walked off.

"Isn't she beautiful?" asked Patti, lovesick.

"She sure is," I said, smitten.

Months later, in July, Mason was well into her fifteenth year, and Patti called panicked. She had to go to the hospital, serious bone infection, did I know of any kennels or anything? She had hardly any money, she didn't know what to do, please help.

Chaos ensued. Mason at my house was disastrous; my

dogs jumped all over her and she almost had a seizure. "Get me outa here right now," her eyes said.

But Mason at a kennel would be even worse. I worked for various rescue kennels. The dogs there go slightly insane. Even with nice runs and good food and fresh water at all times, they're in prison; they hate it. They need to love somebody, preferably a couple of other dogs and a human. They need a sofa and a treat. An old dog, especially an old dog suffering from the loss of her beloved, cannot have any stress if you want her to live.

I phoned Ted, Patti's friend who had only one dog, whom he loved. Sure, bring her over, said Ted.

One month, two months, almost three months passed. Patti was so sick, maybe they were going to amputate a leg. Patti was also heartsick. Alone, in the hospital, she thought nobody cared whether she lived or died. Depression and illness will do that. Also, that very same year Patti had two beloved brothers die. It was way too much for even the strongest of women, which Patti is. She concentrated on her dog. She called Ted for progress reports. So did I.

"She's fine," said Ted. But Mason wasn't really fine.

Let me see if I can say this without being a nasty boogerhead. Some people are morbidly warped and don't like dogs at all. We shall not even discuss such deviants. Some people only love their own dogs, or young cute puppies, or fancy showdogs. These people are dog-impaired, and one must pity them a little. It's like they can see paradise only from the corners of their eyes; when they look straight at it, it's gone.

And then there are the dog-besotted, the dog-goofy, those lunatics who worship at the Holy Church of Canine. I know a woman named Pam who runs a rescue kennel and bailed out of the pound the hugest, sorriest-looking, tumor-covered, nastiest old guy ever alive. She is blissfully in love. My friend Lynn Ann and I take our dogs to the park, and we keep falling against each other with glee as we watch the antics of so many dogs running and humping and eating old french-fry bags. We are the luckiest of humans. We believe fervently in dog, and dog believes back.

So what I think is, Ted is a very nice human, slightly impaired. He got tired and fed up with Mason; she wasn't his dog. Back to square one.

Patti was freaking out. Me too. I boarded Mason for a few days at my vet's office; she said Mason was a little senile but in decent health.

I squinched up my brain for hours on end. Where can an old dog go? Finally I decided. Mason had to go home.

I went to the vet to pick her up. She was standing in her cage, one leg in her water, the other in her food. Her eyes were glazed over and dull. I walked her to my car. She could hardly put one foot in front of the other. No way she could climb into the car. No way she even knew what a car was anymore. I picked her up; she struggled and panicked.

When we got to Patti's apartment building, Mason stood in the yard and started circling. She wouldn't stop. I didn't know what to do, so I brought her inside the apartment and she circled more. With those dazed eyes. No recognition. No nothing.

I got down on the floor with her, stroked her, massaged her. Nothing. Circling. I pulled out some freeze-dried liver. Nothing. Nothing. No, wait. A little sniffing. A slight look of recognition. More sniffing, nose moving to my hand, moving away, moving back. Finally she took the liver, then more. Then circling. Then liver. Then more liver. We did this for over an hour.

Then she went to the door. I opened it. Mason walked

outside, down the wheelchair ramp, over to the grass, and peed. Then she strolled a little, took a dump, walked back up the wheelchair ramp, came inside, went right to her bed and to sleep. She was home.

"I keep remembering her as a puppy," Patti told me on the phone. "We lived in Massachusetts, in farm country. Mason would run around all morning visiting everybody at every farm. She was the happiest little dog. Even when we moved to Los Angeles she used to have her route. She'd go up to Rudy's Cafe, visit all her friends, and cadge treats. I know you don't approve of her running free, and I would never do it now. But I used to go outside, yell, 'Where's my puppy?' and she would come tearing around the corner, so thrilled with herself, a ball of wriggles."

Mason was no ball of wriggles anymore. Dogs have just got to do something about this short life-span thing. It's way too heartbreaking.

For the next three months Lynn Ann and I took shifts going to see Mason three or four times a day. We begged and shamelessly pleaded with everyone we knew to help us. Some days Mason was happy and alert and would be so thrilled to go on her walks her tail would plume up and wag. Sometimes she licked my face daintily. But there were times when she just stood in a corner and stared at nothing, and those times were becoming more frequent.

Patti was going through her own hell. They didn't amputate her leg, but she needed to be transferred to another hospital for an operation and was mired in red tape.

"Don't you dare die before your human gets home," I told Mason. I was frantic, determined that I could keep her alive if I just tried hard enough. Then I would stop, realize what an idiot I was, trying to cheat death.

One day I was sick and decided to hell with the evening visit. When I got there the next morning Mason was lying on her side. I couldn't wake her up. I burst into tears. Mason's eyes opened.

"Oh, God, Mason, I'm sorry I love you please please please," I said.

She decided, for whatever reason, to live a little longer. But it took her days to recover. She needed her routine. She needed everything easy and predictable. She needed me to make her a trail of freeze-dried liver crumbs so she could find her bed.

I spent Christmas Eve and New Year's Eve with Mason. We celebrated in our sedate and dignified way. Patti was coming home on January 3. I wanted to be there for their reunion but thought it would be indelicate.

On January 3, I sat on my hands, waiting for the phone to ring. It didn't. Finally I called Patti. She was sobbing.

"She's not the same dog, she's not even there, she doesn't even know who I am!" Patti cried. "She's just standing and staring off at nothing and there is nothing at all in her eyes. I don't know what to do. Maybe I should just put her out of her misery. Where is my dog?"

Oh, God.

"Listen, Patti," I said. "Even the tiniest bit of stress is too much for her. Give it a couple of days. Please. It will be all right."

The next few days I felt empty and stupid and really sad. I called for progress reports. Mason was a little better. Then a little worse. Then nothing at all for several days. Then a call from Patti, a whole new Patti.

"She's back!" Patti giggled, shrieked, and bubbled. "She remembers me. She's following me everywhere! She remembers her favorite place to pee! She loves her walk! Her eyes are bright and she knows what's going on!"

My eyes filled up and spilled over.

Then there was an even bubblier call. Mason had gone to the beach. Major tail-wagging! She had galloped!

On February 28, Mason was sweet sixteen. I went over to visit.

"This may sound silly," said Patti, "but I never thought I could love her more than I already did, but I love her even more now. For years, she would be my comfort, come up, wag her tail, kiss me, and love me—it was like a drug. And now I'm doing it for her. I'm her comfort. She leans against me, looks to me for everything, and well, jeez, I'm just so nuts about her."

Mason was fabulous. Her coat was gorgeous. She received me graciously, took liver from my fingers with perfect finesse and agility; before it had been a jerky, haphazard grope. We went to Rudy's, her old hangout, her eyes were bright, her step jaunty. But most important, her very essence had changed. Instead of the panicky, nervous, unhappy dog she was while Patti was away, she was a calm girl, a content and relaxed girl.

"Isn't she so precious?" Patti said.

She is more precious than anything. She just kept on keeping on, waiting for her human.

How to Read Your Dog
Danny Shanahan

Over the years, my family and I have had the pleasure of being the loved and loving owners of many dogs. From Lord Jeff, the beautiful and neurotic purebred collie, to the muttish and indifferent, politically incorrect Sambo—each and every one has been instrumental to my education in what I call the Hound Dog Psyche, or, What Gleams the Eye and Wags the Tail. I've always prided myself on being a patient and, I trust, discerning observer of Man's Best Friend. It hasn't always been easy. I have suffered ridicule and scorn, been rebuffed and ignored—once you've been given the canine cold shoulder, it's hard to imagine a shoulder that's colder. But perseverance wins out. Those who have seen the capering curs in my cartoons seem to realize and appreciate this. "You speak their language," is the compliment they often offer. It is an exaggerated and richly undeserved one. I'm no Doolittle: in the final analysis, the canine tongue licks all of us, then licks us all again.

It has come to my attention, however, that the wealth of information I've gleaned throughout my many years of dog watching should not, and cannot, continue to be used solely for its entertainment value and my own financial gain. I must share it with others, and share it freely. Or, if not quite freely, then at least gladly, and at fair market value.

What follows, then, is a brief primer in Dog, consisting of a handful of common mannerisms I've managed to identify and interpret. They are divided into three categories: looks, says, does. The accompanying illustrations are of my own Emma, a gentle and devoted Labrador retriever with a confounding penchant for dry cat food and General Hospital (not necessarily in that order). She was a willing, invaluable collaborator, holding many poses for seconds at a time. I think I speak for both of us when I say our sole reason for constructing this guide is to promote even greater concord and closeness between man (and woman) and dog; if, in doing so, we upset the occasional accepted behavioral applecart, then so be it. Those who would rather play dead than acknowledge the degree of canine complexity I've uncovered, who have no wish to see age-old assumptions and beliefs stewed, chewed, and buried—please, scat.

I. Looks

A. THE HEAD COCK

To assume that dogs who cock their heads (as shown above) are simply listening is a half-truth; to assume they're trying to hear and understand us is something worse. Dogs who cock their heads are engaged in a fierce inner struggle— not merely to comprehend, but to also remain calm and respectful. Were it not for the act of tilting their mugs in mock concentration (usually biting their tongues or the inside of their cheeks as well), they would run the potentially embarrassing risk of laughing—loud, long, uncontrollably— at nearly everything we say to them.

B. THE SAD-EYED LOOK

The Sad-Eyed Look is most often seen on the dog who places his or her head on a couch, chair, windowsill, or knee. It is not a look of sadness, however. It is a look of contemplative pity and compassion, combined. The dog who wears it feels and forgives the cruel mischance of our being born human. "You may be nothing more than a shabby marionette," it says, "but you're my shabby marionette."

C. THE WINK

Many experts foolishly ascribe the wink to the so-called "intelligent" breeds. This is nonsense. All dogs are intelligent; all dogs wink. Their winks at us are a how-dee-do and a thumbs-up; a signal that all's right with their world. Between themselves, however, it's a different story. Winks have many meanings, and are often mis-understood. This usually leads to a brief, vociferous dogfight. Rarely, though, do they end in serious injury. The winner of these altercations, more often than not, will help the loser up, dust him off, pat him on the back, and shake his paw. He'll then offer to buy him a cold one, but not before favoring anyone nearby with a long broad wink.

II. Says

A. THE SHORT YIP

The Short Yip, or Yap, is the "aloha" of the canine lan-guage. Depending on the breed, sex, situation, or mood of the dog in question, it can mean "hello" or "good-bye," "yes" or "no," "say what?" or "muzzle it!" It's frequently used to show annoyance or impatience, and can be, when repeated in an incessant, mind-numbing, machine-gun mantra, extremely effective in driving off burglars, evil spirits, psychoanalysts, and children selling candy bars or magazines.

B. The Long Howl

Expect yet another rise in postal rates, or one more day-time talk show, or both.

C. Whining at the Door

The Door Whine, unlike the Ouch! Whine or the Cat-under-the-Bed Whine, has a much deeper, more sinister meaning. It is an irrefutable red flag: Trouble is coming. It may be a minor inconvenience—a bad check or a bad cold. Or it could be a premonition of something far, far worse. On the Ides of March, many hundreds of years ago, a dog whined at a door. Had the Great Caesar chosen to heed this warning, we all may have ended up drinking wine, eating hummingbird, and living with Martha Stewart. But, as you can probably surmise, the Emperor merely clapped his hands and had the dog let out. He may have thought to avoid a mess in his Great Room; in doing so, he sealed his fate. Et tu?

III. Does
A. Jumping up on People

All dogs are fascinated by clothing—yours, mine, the girl-next-door's. While they may seem to jump up in an apparently joyful, unrestrained show of greeting or affection, they really want to feel fabric, any fabric. To try to break them of this habit is to deprive them of a very sensuous experience. Through the delicate pads on their front paws, they're able to perceive and enjoy rich and varied sensations. Not to mention, judging by recent fashion sensibilities, a marked feeling of superiority.

B. Kicking and Twitching (While Asleep)

Granted, many a dog is dreaming of chasing slow rabbits or earthbound squirrels, but just as many of them are dreaming of chasing a sheepskin, if only we'd let them into our colleges and universities.

C. Kicking and Twitching (While Awake)

The only explanation for this is that your dog has been recently exposed to the early Sun recordings of Elvis Presley. If he hasn't, he should be.

D. Riding with the Head out the Window

Dogs have long endured a shaky, distrustful relationship with cars. A loved one carried off, a trip to the vet, motion sickness, even the specter of sudden death—these are only a few of the memories that contribute to a deep unease in or around automobiles. Any dog who enjoys riding in a car is, in fact, a consummate actor. With his head out the window, he can fill his gray woolly with wind and distractions. Perhaps he'll pretend he's a jet or a chickadee. He can count men with ponytails, or women in black tights. With his feet off the ground and his tongue hanging out, he's

moving full-speed ahead, not sure of where he's going, or whether he'll get there at all. He needs to count people—he's dangerously close to becoming a person himself.

E. Chasing the Tail

This is one of the most common yet least understood aspects of canine behavior. To us, watching an aged, beloved poodle lose his balance and spin into the dry sink or the potted ficus, it seems silly, an exercise in futility. Study it for as long as I have, though, and you'll realize that the Chase is a Zen-like centering activity, capable of transporting and transforming. I've seen dogs who, even after grabbing their tail in their teeth, continued to chase frantically. They'd become a whirling blur, until, with a loud pop, they'd disappear completely. Moments later, they'd blink back into existence, radiating an unmistakable aura of peaceful bliss. Sadly, this is not always the case. I've watched as more than a few unfortunate others chased and chased, then turned, inexplicably, into butter.

Meeting Hobo

Ron Carlson

As I write this, my dog, Max, a twelve-year-old Australian shepherd, sleeps behind me on the carpet. We have our own language, the way close dogs and people have always communicated; most of it is body language, but Max also has five distinct barks (one exclusively for the UPS drivers) that he uses for unambiguous announcements, and he has four variations on the moan/groan, which he uses for amusement, affection, and suggestion. He has guarded my wife and me forever and herded my children from the time they could walk. There is a good chance he thinks they're his. He still patrols our house during gatherings. This past Halloween the boys, now ten and nine, had a party for twenty friends, and Max worked it like a field, nosing kids together or apart, depending on the mood and noise level. We've all tramped the big woods of Utah, where we have a family cabin, and Max has been with me deep into the Wind River Mountains of Wyoming on backpacking trips. Twelve years with a dog is impossible to describe — incalculable,

irreducible. But I know how and why I got him and that is the story I want to tell here.

*

On the third day of snow, we made a mistake.

We'd hung around camp all day tending the small fire, drinking instant coffee thick with powdered milk. From time to time Roger would throw a fly into the riffle where the stream from Grassy Lake fed into Native Lake, or I would go cast into Native, but it was all halfhearted. We had plenty of fish. We wanted it to stop snowing. It was mid-September. We wanted the sun to come out and Indian summer to resume, and stirring anxiously from two and a half days of stamping around in the now foot-deep snow and eight miles from the trailhead at Cold Springs, we made a mistake. We'd made a dozen jokes about how serious this really was, most of them phrased, "From the position of the bodies, it seems the men fought over the last cup of coffee. . . ." I asked Roger if he just wanted to pack it up, and he said he did, and in the even light of midafternoon, the same maddening flat light we'd squinted through for two and a half days, we stuffed the tent and sleeping bags and all the cooking gear we could find into our packs, and we broke camp.

We knew it was too late in the day and we knew that even if we reached the trailhead by dark, that was little help because the snow was knee-deep for 100 miles. But we had to do something; that's what we told ourselves. The snow kept falling. We had to move out.

And then within five minutes we knew it was a mistake. Though the trail was marked with blazes on the trees, they were forty or fifty feet apart, and the actual trail between— as well as potholes, rocks, and other obstacles—was obscured. It was awful. I'd step on the wrong side of a hidden rock and stumble. It became easier to fall than to quickstep and catch myself. We were wet in half an hour, and the only option was to keep moving. Roger and I took turns breaking trail, but we could see we weren't going to make the car by nightfall. We might make the hunters' tent we'd seen hiking up four days before.

At 8:00 P.M., in the last tatters of daylight, in the still-falling snow, we entered the big, open meadow called Hayes Park. We were still two miles from the car and what was the point anyway? We'd made a mistake. We should have stayed in camp and had soup and waited this big weather out. The trail cut down the middle of Hayes Park, and with no trees and no blazes, we simply lost the trail and started blundering down the snowfield in the new dark. We were falling every tenth step because of the uneven terrain.

Halfway down Hayes Park, I realized Roger was not with me, and I turned to find him 200 yards back. He was standing still. I called. He just stood. I dropped my head, turned, and stamped back to him. His forehead was wet with sweat and his eyes were swollen. He looked at me darkly. "Come on," I said. "Half a mile to the bottom of the park and we'll camp in the elk hunters' lodge we saw."

Roger shook his head. Something wasn't right here. "Come on," I said. "We can make it." He shook his head and swore. He didn't seem himself. We had an argument, the punch line of which was him saying, "You go ahead." I thought it over: From the position of their bodies, it seems the one partner left the other one in Hayes Park.

We needed some soup, some noodles, some coffee. It was decided that we would cut over into the woods and camp.

My old friend Roger is an excellent outdoorsman and the best firekeeper I've ever encountered. We kicked an eight-foot circle as clear as we could and while I broke dead limbs from the nearby pines, Roger knelt and started a tiny fire. Each limb snapped off in the cold with a crack that stung my hands, but it was the kind of chore that has a powerful sense of utility about it. Every one of these limbs was going to burn. We weren't talking, just working. Roger fed the fire up and we fell to cooking, melting snow for tomato soup and Tang and instant coffee and then macaroni-and-cheese and more coffee. The fire opened a spreading circle of the forest floor, green grass and little wildflowers that had been our company four days earlier. Roger warmed up and apologized for having to stop. We talked about tomorrow. The snow had thinned to a periodic shower of tiny tiny flakes. We'd just get to the car and then figure something out. The car was twelve miles from the road.

We stood the freestanding tent on the snow a little later and climbed in. I remember it as a night I just wanted to be home in my own bed in Salt Lake; I was worried. We weren't in real trouble, but the next few days were going to be tough, at least.

Sometime after 2:00 A.M. I was awakened by shaking, which I couldn't figure out. Roger was trembling with chill. It took me a full minute to wake him—his shivering was persistent. His face was swollen again, and I realized in a second that he had not changed clothes at all and he lay there wet and possibly hypothermic. It was cold. I sat him up and pulled off his parka. He was breathing through his teeth but nodding at me. He peeled off his soaked shirts, and we put the jacket back on him and sealed him back in his bag. A moment later the last wave of trembling subsided. Later still, I slept.

The next morning I saw the sweetest thing: shadows on the tent. The sun was out. Then I heard a noise we would hear on and off all day, a kind of muted crash as clumps of snow fell in bunches from the trees. We took extra time with the restoked fire, eating our oatmeal and coffee and then packing with care. The sun and the snow now brilliant, the world brilliant, gave new heart to our trek, and we stopped to take some photographs.

Walking in Hayes Park still was a kind of treachery, though we fell less often. At the bottom of the meadow we found the white canvas hunters' tent, and there was smoke coming from the stovepipe through the roof. We hollered and a voice came back. Of all the instances of irony I've met, entering that tent represents the most prominent. It was a huge dry space with two stoves, one bleating out heat. The coffee was on. Our host was a young guy from Steven's Point, Michigan. We had a cup with him in that warm tent and then went on our way. We'd slept in the snow 400 yards west, and Roger and I exchanged one glance about that and it was enough.

Two hours later we came into the clearing at Cold Springs, the trailhead. Roger's car was buried under the two-foot snow, but we found it and, after a struggle, cleared it off and pushed it back one car length, revealing a dry spot for our tent. Cold Springs is on the eastern slope of the Wind River Range, and at almost ten thousand feet we could see half of western Wyoming laid out under the bright snow. The highway was twelve snowy miles east. Here we were on the edge of the Wind River Indian Reservation, and cattle in twos and threes dotted the white hillside. We didn't know what we were going to do, but we decided to rest for the day, get good and dry, and think about trekking out tomorrow. It would be heavy going, but it was downhill.

I remember that day well. I cleared an area near the car and sat in the little circle of snow out of the wind. The sun was steady, and I took off my shirt and read from a book of stories I'd brought, *Twenty Grand,* thinking, people in Sun Valley pay $500 a day for this.

That night we had a big dinner in the early dark and sat by the fire, making plans. Neither one of us wanted to walk out. We had the wrong shoes and were sick of being wet and cold. But we knew it would be weeks before this early snow would clear enough to make it easier. There was no question about the car; we'd have to return later. So we steeled ourselves to it; it would be a long day, but we'd walk. At least the tent was on dry ground tonight.

Just before we turned in, we heard a rustling and a dog burst into the circle of firelight. It was a brindled, tailless shepherd of some kind with snow frozen to his hackles. He checked us out and then, hearing his master's voice in the distance, bounded away. Five minutes later two men came up. They were John, a wildcatter from Rawlins, and his buddy Richard, an accountant from Cheyenne. They'd been out to climb Gannet, the highest peak in Wyoming, but had been rejected by the weather. Their truck was the other lump in the snow. Did we want to walk out tomorrow and hitch to Lander? We could take turns breaking trail, and with four of us, it might not be so bad. We stoked up the fire and talked it over. We decided to go for it. The dog came up and sat by the fire. He was an Australian shepherd and his name was Hobo.

The next day was my birthday, September 15, and it dawned frigid, clear, and still. Our gear was ready and we packed lightly, leaving the tent and our sleeping bags and pads in the car. Richard and John came over from where they'd camped, and we started down. We wanted to make the road before dark so we could try to get a ride. The mood was what? Serious. I simply felt serious.

It was obvious the dog loved the snow, leaping ahead of us as we formed our single file. John had told me Hobo was just an apartment dog, that he'd never really been out this way before. Then the strangest thing happened. Hobo took off. John called, but the dog was gone. I wasn't used to dogs and didn't know what to think. I was trying to watch the trail that those ahead of me had kicked, so I wouldn't get my feet too wet too early. Then Hobo came back, but with company. We all stood still, four men in the first rays of the sun in a white world, while Hobo nipped and barked at three cattle, herding them over to us and then downhill. We followed. Then Hobo was off again, gathering another cow and a calf, and then back

and then off to bring back four more steers. The single line of cattle led us down the buried dirt road, Hobo adding to the line every minute or two. It was stunning. The sun rose and grew warm, and the light packs were a pleasure. The trail was like a paved road, the snow packed flat, and we walked easily down this broad sidewalk without getting wet. John got out his camera and the day became a kind of holiday, the kind of walk I'll never take again. By noon we could see the road, and by one o'clock we walked out onto Wyoming Route 287. The sixty cattle Hobo had gathered stood at the fence and watched us. We rode in the back of a pickup to Crowheart and there, at the general store, four people headed for a wedding in Denver squeezed us into the backseat of a Wagoneer. Hobo got in the far back and lay down. One of the women turned and said, "Well, you've been up there almost a week. Did you know Grace Kelly died?"

We would spend that night in Lander, Wyoming, in a motel, with Hobo sleeping on the floor. The next night Roger and I would board a westbound train in Rawlins and take it to Ogden, Utah. I have a photograph of the two of us in the dining car. My wife, Elaine, met us at the station at eleven that night with a magnificent and extended train-station embrace, and we told her the story driving home. I only knew Hobo two days.

*

And now Max is twelve and in a way I'm twelve too. Elaine went out that year and found me an Australian shepherd pup who has walked a million steps with me and slept a thousand hours by my bed. All I'll say now about any of it is simple: My gratitude to Hobo covers all these years. He saved a day a long time ago and so many more since.

Stan Olson

All I have to do is turn the knob on the closet door where I keep my outdoor stuff and Patsy is immediately in the hall with me and remains underfoot as I dress and get our gear ready. Like any good dog she is always up for a walk, but she knows that the closet means we're going to the country.

When I'm dressed and ready to go, with Patsy's field bag on my shoulder, I casually say, "I thought I'd go for a long walk in the country, and if you're not doing anything I'd love for you to join me." There's no reason for this, of course, but it amuses me.

When we drive, Patsy lies on the seat next to me, always with her head away from me (or maybe it's with her butt toward me, and knowing her that's a distinct possibility) and I rest my hand on her back.

I particularly like going out with her when there is snow, as her tracks make an interesting diagram of her activity.

When I walk in the country with Patsy she finds things I don't see

old bottle

F R O G

T U R T L E

snake

woodcock

Binoculars

Patsy's field bag:

LEASH
WATER
WHISTLE
MED. KIT (DOG)
SNACKS (DOG)
BIRD I.D. BOOK

Why don't you just get in the car and take us out there?

I'D LOVE FOR YOU TO JOIN ME.

Standard Wellies

Fetch

Jane Smiley

Not too long ago, on one of those windy cool days that make horses spooky and self-willed, I was standing with my gray Thoroughbred gelding, Tick Tock, in the grassy field outside the barn, letting him graze and snort at shadows after his bath. When suddenly he threw his head up, I looked around to discover that his great and good friend, another Thoroughbred gelding named Ace, had pushed out of his stall door and was happily trotting out of the barn toward us. Tick Tock started backing and pulling on the lead rope I was holding, and Ace, after greeting Tick Tock with a whinny and a snort, began to gallop around us in large circles, veering toward trees, toward the house, toward the road, all the while half scared by the wind and half exultant at his freedom. Tick Tock immediately took his mood. Knowing that the two big horses were certainly more than I could handle, I began calling for my trainer, Gail, whose hurry from the horse pasture was slowed by her broken toe. She rounded the house just in time to watch, appalled, with me, horrified, as Ace headed straight for the triple clothesline, which he couldn't see. We both gasped, but just at the last moment, apparently feeling

the first wire with his ears or head, Ace ducked under, slid to the left of the poles, and came on at a gallop, even more excited but not yet any worse for the wear. Tick Tock continued to back and curve, jerking at the lead rope. I was crooning, "Whoa, Tick Tock, whoa, baby." Gail, now carrying a bucket of grain, was calling, "Come here, Ace, come here, old boy." He came and was caught. Tick Tock watched him go, settled down, and went back to grazing. I caught my breath and looked down at my feet, where my golden retriever, Amber, had just dropped her ball for me to throw. At no time during the whole brouhaha of trampling and galloping hooves, shouting humans, and blowing winds had Amber lost sight of her mission, which was to pick up her ball, carry it a few steps, and drop it hopefully at my feet. Now that's what I call genius.

Before we got Amber, the family ball-handler was our Great Dane, Hitchcock, who would fetch a ball or Frisbee, and was even willing to catch one in his mouth if you lobbed it in there as easily as you could, rather the way you might lay up a basketball. But Hitchcock really didn't see any point to it, and he got bored after more than a few throws. He was a good dog, like our sheltie (now there was a dog with no interest in balls—a ball could roll past his nose and he wouldn't even lift his head off the floor), easy to housebreak and obedience train, attentive to us, few vices. But Great Danes are above tricks and resolute about the irrelevance of swimming to the life of an intelligent canine.

I wasn't thinking "retriever" when I bought Amber. I was thinking "replacement for lost cat." She was nine weeks old and ready to go—none of that separation despair I Iitchcock showed when we brought him home. She was outgoing, self-confident, and full of energy from the moment we took her out of the car. We carried her into the yard. My husband tossed a stick. Amber scrambled after it, a rusty-gold ball of fluff with a tiny little bark and teeth like tacks.

By the time she got a little leg on her, at, say, sixteen weeks, there was nothing she could not do with a ball. Chase it, find it, catch it in the air, hold it between her paws and let it fall into her mouth, swim for it, even dive for it. Keeping her eye on the ball wasn't a skill for her, it was an inner compulsion. You could not divert her attention from a ball by making loud noises, calling her name, or even offering her food. Given the choice between eating her dinner and fetching a ball, Amber will always go for the ball—and that is saying something, because she's been clocked at forty-two seconds downing her kibble.

Throwing the ball for her soon gave me an eerie and even uncomfortable feeling. A Great Dane is not unlike your average human, a generalist who over the centuries has been taught to engage in various activities, from guarding to killing wild boar to cleaning up the scraps under medieval banquet tables. But it was clear from the beginning that Amber was not in control of what moved her. To show her a ball was to gain absolute power over her. Her eyes would focus, her body would tense, nothing you might say or do would wipe that look off her face, that look of pure concentration. She seemed machinelike to me, and the only thing that reassured me was her *joie de vivre*. Her every day seemed filled with the delight of being a dog.

As she matured, she came to remind me of other geniuses I'd known or heard of. Of course, her performance in her chosen field was both sustained and remarkable. I don't think she's ever failed to find a thrown ball, for instance. She'll return to the house with it long after everyone else has lost interest, that time spent tirelessly circling the area until her goal is achieved. She can come back days later to a ball left on the trail, showing all the signs of having remembered it and looked forward to having it again in her mouth. No ball is too dirty or disgusting to be picked up, either. If a ball is in a closed cupboard or out of sight on a high shelf, Amber will sit, pointing her nose directly at it, until it is given to her or she hears the "no ball!" command. There are few bounces she can't predict the trajectory of. When she is in the mood, she apparently feels no pain. The hard "thwock" of a ball into her throat does not faze her. If it bounces off her nose, which surely must hurt, she goes after it without missing a beat. Once, she crossed in front of my husband just as he was swinging his driver, and he drove the golfball into her hip. Her only reaction was to whip after it and catch it on the rebound. She is no longer taken fishing, because sometimes she can't resist jumping for the lure, even though she's been told not to over and over.

Here's what I've learned from Amber: Genius is inbred and comes on early. Genius finds its object. Genius is inventive; when Amber can't get anyone to play with her, she drops the ball down the stairs and fetches it for herself. Once I saw her get an Airedale puppy to play catch with her. She would toss the ball toward the puppy, who would pick it up and then drop it. Amber would run after it joyfully, then back off and toss it again. Genius knows no hierarchies or territories; Amber will fight for balls with older male dogs on their turf—she claims all balls for her own. Genius is not intelligence (she was no easier to housebreak or train than the other dogs), but rather a profound desire coupled with a compelling aesthetic sense; when Amber sees a ball, she wants to do what she knows ought to be done with it. Amber and her genius possess each other—we have often noticed that a willing ball thrower can drive her to exhaustion. We have to stop her for her sake, because she will not stop for her own.

Of course, Amber's genius has been intentionally bred into her. Sometimes I wonder about the ethics of this, especially when she acts a little strangely—for example, when a much-loved human comes home, and, rather than run to the door in greeting, Amber goes straight to the ball shelf, her affectionate joy immediately associating the loved person and the loved object. But finally you have to envy her, because she is never without a purpose in life, never bored, never unsure of herself as long as there is a tennis ball, or a golf ball, or an apple, or a snowball, or even a basketball somewhere around, because if she can't pick it up, at least she can roll it.

Timothy Greenfield-Sanders

Forty years ago my parents bought me and my older brother, Charles, two beagles. Our younger brother, Frank, had just been born and they thought we might be jealous of him, so along came Foffy and Rennie. Foffy was my dog. I can still vividly remember sitting on the floor of the station wagon with my new puppy as we drove home from the farm where he was born.

Foffy lived for fifteen wonderful years, my entire childhood. Toward the end of his life Foffy lost his judgment about food. He ate everything and far too much of it. Years later, when my first child, Isca, was born, her eating habits mirrored those of Foffy in his dotage. Before long, Isca was nicknamed Foffy. Eventually we had to explain to Isca why she had been nicknamed after my childhood dog. Fortunately, all Foffys have a fine sense of the ridiculous and a marvelous sense of humor.

These days my contact with dogs is through my artist friends. The following are some of my favorite dog portraits.

MINI (ROSS BLECKNER'S DACHSHUND).

FRANKIE Frankie, whose nickname is Franklin, is a just-grown combination poodle-Yorkshire terrier. Inexhaustibly playful, his favorite pastime is imitating Estelle Parsons having hysterics.

Frankie was rescued from the oven of a local Long Island pound by the North Shore Animal League. The very day before, I had implored my friend Marge Stein, North Shore's patient publicist, to find me an adorable dog, preferably purebred, even more shamelessly promising her a plug in Cindy Adams's column. "That's not necessary," replied an incredulous Marge, adding her recently coined slogan Love Needs No Pedigree! She called the next day to tell me about Frankie, whimsically linking him to her idol Frank Sinatra, who is eternally bussing one of North Shore's precious pooches in a photo that hangs prominently in her office.

I may have moxie for a fey creature, but I always deliver the goods, and though I have a feeling the closest Mrs. Adams ever got to an animal is a sable coat, she is a loyal and supportive friend who duly plugged not only North Shore and Franklin, but in the same item ingeniously included Mr. Sinatra, novelist Rona Jaffe, and an East Side Cantonese restaurant. . . .

—BEAUREGARD HOUSTON-MONTGOMERY

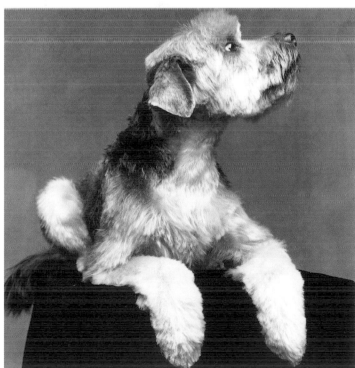

TIMOTHY GREENFIELD-SANDERS
CLOCKWISE FROM TOP LEFT: MARSDEN (ROBERT GREENE'S STANDARD POODLE), MIES (RONALD JONES'S DACHSHUND),
FRANKIE (BEAUREGARD HOUSTON-MONTGOMERY'S POODLE/YORKIE MIX), RASCAL (MATTHEW WEINSTEIN'S DOG).

TIMOTHY GREENFIELD-SANDERS
ARCHIE (ROBERT ROSENBLUM AND JANE KAPLOWITZ'S BULLDOG).

TRUE ROMANCE Another story, this, about life imitating art. In 1988 I published The Dog in Art from Rococo to Post-Modernism, an art-historical caprice that readers may well have been deceived into thinking was written by someone who had always shared his life with dogs. But that, I now write with embarrassment, is a total falsehood. As far as dogs went, I was a bachelor until 1990, when my book came to life in a new twist on the Pygmalion and Galatea story.

The epiphany was simple and sudden, and having checked my diary I can now date it precisely. In the entry for September 23, I jotted (apparently after the fact, for he came to us namelessly) "Archie arrives." My two children, of course, had been nagging all along for a dog, and so had my wife; but I kept putting my foot down, repeating the dull litany of reasons for remaining liberated from a self-inflicted burden. Then, on that eventful Sunday, while I was out of town for the afternoon, the three of them went off to join some dog-nut friends at an annual bulldog convention in western Connecticut. One thing, it's true, had been clear. by unanimous vote, the English bulldog was our favorite breed. But I preferred to experience its irresistibly grotesque charm in the undemanding and uninvolving form of, say, the bulldog portraits by Delaroche or Toulouse-Lautrec. I still recall the shock, then, of putting the key in the lock to discover behind the door a squealing family surprise party. With a large dark spot like a pirate's around one eye, there, fallen from the sky, was a white bulldog puppy (born, I was quickly told, on Bastille Day, just two months

before), and it was waiting, so they thought, for my instant surrender. But my inflamed ego—how dare they do this behind my back?—made the anonymous intruder almost unlovable for about twenty-four hours. And that is the short first act of an epic romance that will go beyond the grave.

The next day, of course, all began to change. By the time this stranger became Archie (the children didn't cotton to the arty, classical names—Atlas, Ajax, Hector, Hyacinth—we tossed into the ring, but Archie finally got all our votes), I was totally happy that my unsmiling prediction, that I would be the only one to take care of him, came true. And I am still happy, four years later, when the life-enhancing rhythms of walking Archie three times a day (early morning, late afternoon, and just before bedtime) and feeding him twice a day (just after our breakfast and before our dinner) continue to be absorbed into my own mental and physical metabolism, where they provide the kind of mysterious serenity that, way back in the 1970s, I recall toying with in the form of one of the decade's spiritual fashions, transcendental meditation. Who needs twice-a-day, eyes-closed, inward voyages when you can slip into oblivion by becoming one with a sixty-pound teddy bear of a mantra who looks like a canine Popeye (mammoth biceps and pectorals followed by a bell-jar waist), understands your every mood shift and has as many of his own, and participates in a mystical fusion with subhuman (or is it superhuman) sensations?

I never stop marveling over the strange release of near-psychoanalytic dimensions that Archie can trigger in his thrice-daily rounds of Greenwich Village, where we live. A very doggy neighborhood, it is filled with people who walk id-first, barely restrained by a leash. We all follow our temporary masters as they do things Freud taught us lie not so far below the surface of our own two-legged, upright stances — sniffing strangers' pudenda, wallowing in a scatological continuum, or, less carnally, merely insisting that this is mine and not yours. And then there is the ventriloquial stunt. I am constantly amazed by all these strangers who, like me, talk through their dogs. I know few of these people's names; and should we bump into each other dogless, we refer only hurriedly to our canine personae, squirming with the momentary exposure of our human selves. But when protected by our dogs, we go on and on, as if on a shrink's couch. "Good morning, Archie. Here's your friend Lucie, the slut. Watch her turn on her back for you." (And she does.) Might this really be a conversation between the owners? Or just the other day, a new dog on the block is nervously introduced as follows: "Oh, Betty hates males. . . . I must say, don't blame her." Then there's the ultrapampered bichon frise, whose bristly, old-maid mistress always salutes with a warning: "Archie, don't come near her. You weigh too much and you'll hurt her. Besides, she just had a bath." And invariably, there is the wordless ventriloquist in black leather whose Doberman growls at Archie like Cerberus while his owner chillingly avoids my anxious gaze. But apart from these ongoing encounters is the more isolated therapy of a back-to-nature immersion in that cosmos of sensory data — especially via twitching nostrils, which we can only experience vicariously as we are dragged this way and that by the clue of a scent we know is there — right on city pavements, even on the corner of Sixth Avenue — but are too handicapped to perceive.

Back home, Archie takes on another persona, fulfilling now the broadest spectrum of intimate domestic needs as he closes the door on his outdoor life. Family feud? One has only to hold up Archie's hugely compassionate, Buddha-like head to reduce us all to smiles and tears of reconciliation. Feeling down? He is ready to share and to console, with searching eyes and warming body. Tired of adult constraints? Baby talk won't embarrass him. Want to feel significant? Try his whirling-dervish greeting when you return from an overnight trip.

Now I remember the pre-Archie moment when I was doing research for my "dog in art" book and read how Lord Byron was so smitten with Boatswain, his beloved Newfoundland, that he commemorated his grief over the animal's death in 1808 not only with a poem, but with a commission for a funerary monument in which he himself also planned to be buried. At the time, I thought this was a textbook example of the delirious extravagance of the Romantic imagination. Today, however, I am eternally grateful to Archie for giving me the occasion, in an otherwise temperate life, to understand with the heart and not the mind that I, too, can be Byronic. —ROBERT ROSENBLUM

TIMOTHY GREENFIELD-SANDERS
CLOCKWISE FROM TOP LEFT: BEBOP (ISCA AND JOOP SANDER'S DOG), SNOOPS AND BUSTER (LISA PHILLIPS'S DACHS-
HUNDS), CHANEL (ELAINE STURTEVANT'S SOFT-COATED WHEATEN TERRIER), ROSE AND LOUISE (JOHN GUARE'S PUGS).

117

MY SHIH TZU/MY SELF   I wasn't looking for a dog when I met Bongo. I don't know about you, but I assume most people first decide to have a dog and then go about finding the desired breed, size, sex, and color they want. Bongo, however, came with his owner—a professional drummer (hence the name Bongo)—for tea one day, and I never looked back.

I had to have him, this puppy who in one movement touched my pet-free heart. My friend and I had moved away from him. We were sitting, talking, when I looked up to see Bongo, his jaws clasped to the corner of the towel on which I had set a water bowl, dragging it toward us. "He has separation anxieties," I said, naming my own problem.

I dreamed about him after that. I knew the drummer was a wanderer, who, like most musicians, could forget to come home for days. In my dreams, I would stand outside his window in Greenwich Village and talk to Bongo through the grating, knowing he was in there alone, maybe without food and suffering the worst possible anxieties. Our anxiety of being left. I had never dreamed about a dog before.

When the drummer went away on weekend gigs, I would plead for Bongo for a sleepover. I took him everywhere, this golden ball of fluff who never failed to stir the coldest heart.

"You know, he is a spirit, not a real dog," people would confide, as if I didn't know.

The day the drummer announced he was moving to Chicago and that he was giving Bongo to some nice family in the suburbs, I said I had to have him. "But you're always on airplanes!" he said. "You shouldn't have a dog!" I told him that if he didn't give me this animal I would never speak to him again. I said it with every intention of going down and stealing him if my demand wasn't met.

For nine years now Bongo and I have flown together. He goes to the West Coast, to Europe, and has been to Key West so often he gets frequent flyer miles. He sits at my feet while I write. Indeed, I find his company so satisfying that I have made excuses to cancel dinner because I need an evening with him, prefer it.

The saying goes that pets and their owners grow to look alike. Bongo and I grow more psychologically alike. He knows my moods, my thoughts, and if I am ill, he lies against the hurting place. Some people choose a pet as a narcissistic extension, a proud borzoi to show off their own elegance, a King Charles spaniel to elevate their status. Bongo is my Même Chose, my great aunt Betsy's nickname for her favorite daughter, who was like her, inside, not out. My stepfather laughs and says when he comes back in the next life he wants to be my dog. Wise man.   —NANCY FRIDAY

TIMOTHY GREENFIELD-SANDERS
DONGO (NANCY FRIDAY'S SHIH TZU).

Twenty Questions

Lee K. Abbott

A dozen years ago now, in a letter that went merrily along about most of the subjects under high heaven that men and women fret about, my mentor—a man as famous for the glint of his gold incisor and the maddening twinkle in one eyeball as he is for an approach to prose that rivals Attila's to land acquisition—gave me the lowdown on dogs. He had a dog himself, a sloppy monster from the retriever family, an animal straight out of a nightmare from, oh, John Cheever, so I figured he knew what the dickens he was typing about. He'd been my teacher, after all, so I, ever the dutiful student, perked up—yup, doglike. Dogs, he said, only asked two questions of the world: Can I eat it, or will it eat me?

I was amused, of course, but I remember thinking then—because I've a mind also full of questions and wise-guy answers—that maybe my old pal was wrong. In particular, I wondered about—how to put this delicately?—butt-sniffing. As in Rover, bounding through the park one day and, having spied a Fifi-like creature in the distance, bringing himself up short, head cocked, expression curious,

tail already on the wag. I figured then, as in part I figure now, that this beast, driven by eons of instinct, was asking himself something on the order of the following: "Hey, now, I wonder what that's all about. Let's take a look-see. Shoot, let's boogie!" And off he races, in his mind a "hunger" of an equally irresistible kind.

Lately, however, because writing on the subject has obliged me to focus on my generally crosswise experience with dogs, I've come up with a fourth question, likewise relevant to matters of life as lived among the canines I've known. All the dogs you'll read about here—from Chockie, my first, to Al, my most recent; from wild dogs in the street to a drowning dog in a state park—they've all had, alas, one question that desperately needs answering: "Is Lee Abbott in the neighborhood?"

*

Chockie wasn't my dog. Not really. In the time all this takes place, the late fifties and early sixties, he belonged to our neighbors, the Bergers, as fine an example of the textbook nuclear family as you were then likely to stumble across in the deserts of New Mexico where we lived. We, on the other hand, were as bent and damaged a tribe as any that nowadays shows up on Oprah to shed blood between commercials. My mother was a drunk, finally institutionalized; my father, whose work for the United States Army mostly involved golf tournaments and various mischief on the missile range, spent most of his time at the country club. Hence, my brother and I were largely left to our own screwy devices. Minor vandalism. Window-peeping at Marsha Elliot's house. Clod fights at the irrigation canal behind our house. Double features at the State theater. And books, from Faulkner to Genet, that no kid has any business believing.

Best of all, I had Chockie, a pound dog. Ugly as the day after Christmas. Brown as dirt from a melon patch. Wiry and small and fast and forgiving in all matters human—just the pal, in short, for a kid, owing to a home life gone blooey, who would go hysterically blind for a day, or throw a punch through the door to his fourth-grade class, or bail out of the Easter play a minute before show time. Lordy, I went everywhere with that animal—to "A" Mountain and the Rio Grande, west of us, to the desert on my bike, to swim at Charles Sanders's house. You saw me during this period, you saw Chockie. Heck, the Bergers even let him spend the night a few times—just the pair of us in my room, me with a book I didn't know 50 percent the words of, him at my shoulder dreaming of beef bones. Yeah, best friends.

Then came the day I'm partly here to tell about. (In the life of a writer, folks, there always comes a day, one that as ordinary citizen you'd just as soon avoid.) I was in my last year of Little League—a damned good center fielder, by the way—and Chockie and I were roughhousing on the lawn in front of the Bergers' place. We were growling, jumping at each other, wrestling—the play boys are given to and, in part, by which they find out where in the world the lines are drawn. After a time we stopped, tuckered, the two of us regarding the street. Across the way the Coffmans were washing their car; up the road somebody was honking for Nancy Bledsoe, a high school girl I spent at least an hour a day yearning for. I had a game in an hour, so I was wearing my uniform (the Red Sox, naturally; this was before Angels and Mariners and Rangers, not to mention everything else that makes the past virtually unrecognizable to the sentimentalist I sometimes am). The sun was right out of the *Odyssey*, the sky as blue as one painted for postcards. Life, in short, was good: a boy and "his" dog. America as fetched up for you by Norman Rockwell and the speechwriters for Dan Quayle.

Then I got bit. Hard and angrily. On the nose. Evidently, I had done something—an accident, to be sure, but something that nonetheless spooked Chockie. I was on all fours, him sitting beneath me, when he struck. Needless to say, and in the way all such stories seem to work themselves out in my life, I don't remember much after this. I do remember standing, Chockie still affixed to my face, and moving toward my house, thirty feet away. For a moment or two, the pain seemed bearable. I was at once amazed and frightened, at once at the whirling center of this drama and somewhere yonder looking down. Then, crying and yelling, I returned completely to myself, blood squirting down my shirtfront, Chockie still hanging on, his eyes as fierce and intolerant as those belonging to hounds you hear about from hell.

Somewhere in here he let go. Somewhere in here I went in my back door, got my father away from the TV. Somewhere in here we ended up at the emergency room.

And somewhere in here our family doctor, Leland Evans, himself a notorious linkster and tippler, flushed my wounds with saline and said, within my hearing, that, doggone it, we ought to let the mess heal on its own. No stitches. Just some ointments. Bandages. One nostril had been, well, ravaged. The other gouged. A lip had somehow gotten involved. Plus a cheek. And then, too many hours later, we were home, and Chockie, erstwhile best friend, was, according to my dad, out of my life forever.

Truth to tell, I don't remember what happened to Chockie. The Bergers were still our friends. Life went on as it had before—talk across the carports, Sunday lasagna dinners, weeding the nut grass in the massive concrete planter our properties shared. But Chockie was, sadly, no longer in the picture. He was indoors. Or out with Charlie, the son. Which, more truth to tell, was just dandy with me, for I'd discovered that, at twelve years old and with school starting soon, I was scared shitless of dogs—all of them, even Mr. Disney's Pluto.

They meant me harm, I thought. Worse yet, they knew I was a scaredy-cat and, at the very least, they, big and small analogues of Chockie himself, would torment me, and thus I would spend the rest of my life—a century, I thought then—crossing the street or not going down that alley or looking long and hard into the darkness lest somewhere, on the stoop, in the backyard, even on a leash, another beast had his eye on the very meat of me.

*

Which brings me, umpteen umpteens later, to Phideaux (that's Fido to those of you who didn't learn your "animule" names, as I did, from the party records of Justin Wilson—Jooo-STAN Wil-SONE—a Cajun cutup now more cele-brated for cooking than for comedy). Phideaux came into my life during the second year of my four-year courtship of my wife. We were in college. It was December, the dog a miniature French poodle that supposedly was to be a gift for Pam's distant stepsister. You know the rest, I'm sure: A bond develops, time passes, Christmas morning rolls around, and, happy days, it's all been a wonderful charade. The dog, ladies and germs, is yours!

And for nearly eleven years it was as much a part of our family as our two boys. To Pam, Sherrie—the fussy name I could never bring myself to utter—was companion, sleepmate, play pal, the works. To the boys, as they grew, it was the same: delightful as a day in a toy store, good-tempered as the Pope, steadfast as Tonto. Goodness gracious, I even liked the thing: It came when I called, rode in my lap in the car, never pooped on the floor, brought the ball back directly, and seemed tickled to see me every time I came back from the grocery store. It licked, howled in glee, and understood enough English to be a confidante when the sun went down. Yeah, I admit it: I loved the beast, and it, I had every reason to hope, loved me. Immoderately, the way the poor love moola.

Then, the way it is in storybooks, comes another day. Rather, a night. This was in Cleveland Heights, Ohio, 1977, our first year in that special corner of the world. I'd gotten—at twenty-nine, my father liked snidely to point out—my first real job, an assistant professorship at Case Western Reserve University. We'd moved in to the bottom floor of a double on the day Elvis died. I was teaching, bringing home a modest wage, trying to write my way up the heap that literary fame is. Noel and Kelly were in second grade and kindergarten, respectively; Pam was holding down a full-time job.

Thanks to a colleague who came to rescue us, we'd survived a blizzard, our first encounter with snow measured in feet, wind in scary miles per hour. On the page, if not in the home, I was finding the "voice" several strangers now know me by. In the classroom, I was making sense two sentences out of three. The living, so the story goes, was easy. The fish were jumping. Somewhere the cotton was high.

Then it was spring, and I was back to my old habits: staying at home in the afternoon and evening for the boys and returning to my office at seven or so, well after dinner and at the point where the kids seemed headed bedward, to write the fiction my wonts were driving me toward. One night I got home later than usual. It was dark as the cape a witch wears, black as Phideaux herself. For reasons that continue to mystify, I braked the car in the drive. I didn't plan to go out again; indeed, I had no reason to. I was home time to frolic and watch what America had on TV that night. So, after a second or two, I started the car and began pulling it toward the garage in the back of the property. Whereupon, because this is a tragedy, I felt a bump.

Unbeknownst to me, Pam had let Phideaux out, and, very probably recognizing the car, that poodle had scampered out of the bushes to say howdy. At some level deep in the bones, a level I have insufficient intelligence to understand, I knew what had happened—I'd run over my own dog—but the certainty of it, as dread and profoundest horror, didn't occur to me until I was walking back from the garage. There, in the darkness, was a more concentrated, thicker darkness. Phideaux/Sherrie. Crushed dead by her thick-witted master. I didn't say anything as I stood over her. I didn't have any words, only syllables that stand for sadness and regret and fear, some of which became at least one

whole if strangled sentence when I went inside to tell my wife, and our children, that I'd killed the finest beast they'd known.

As I tell the story now to friends and folks, what followed then was a comedy of the blackest sort. My family in hysterics, tears and wailing of the sort you see in Palestine. Me on the phone to one animal shelter or veterinarian after another. Yes, the dog was dead. Sorry, I heard, we only tend to live animals. Yes, the dog was ours. Sorry, another said, we only pick up strays. Sorry. Sorry. So very, very sorry. Finally, after more than two hours, I found myself again on the phone with the animal warden for our suburb. He was sympathetic, understanding, as good a soul as Old King Cole himself. He just couldn't, he said. A violation of the rules. Please, I begged. I'm sure he could hear the weeping behind me. A moment passed. Another. On the other side of town, too late at night to be civilized, a mind was being made up. Maybe he had dogs himself, I thought. Maybe he had a family, like my own, hurtling toward collapse.

Okay, he said at last. Wrap the dog in a towel. Put it in a box at the corner of the house. In the backyard. Tomorrow, before anybody got home, it would be gone. Our secret.

*

Which brings me to the current mutt-in-residence: Al (short for Alex, itself short for Alexandra) the Wonder Dog, she of the five-inch snout and the five-foot vertical leap.

A lot of years, nearly fourteen, passed between Phideaux and Al. The boys grew and were, at a variety of places, educated. Pam worked a variety of jobs. I published books, told on paper a hundred artful lies that some kindly editors paid cash dollars to print. Throughout, we were dogless. By choice. We were busy, went the story we told ourselves. And gone a lot. At best, having an animal would be unfair. At worst, neglectful. So we got cats, Sandy and Peachy; each half Persian, half orange as Halloween. Pets that could fend for themselves, one of which has grown up to be angry and given to fits.

Then, in 1990, the year after we moved to Columbus to take up work as it is organized by honest-to-goodness Buckeyes, I came home from school to find, golly, Al. A black-and-white something-or-other. Part fox terrier, maybe. Part circus act. Pam and Kelly, then a sophomore in high school and in need of a companion, had visited the pound. Up and down one aisle they'd traipsed. In cage A, what could be, after sixty bucks and several signatures, ours. In cage B, another. In cage C, a third. And so on. Al had come to the bars, I was told. She seemed to smile. Her tail thumped. Who could resist? An hour later, she was at my feet, chewing my socks and romping sideways through the family room. Twenty minutes later, I was in love.

I had forgotten about all the other dogs I'd crossed paths with over the years: the pack of mangy beasts I'd driven into the middle of late one night in Las Cruces, New Mexico; the one I'd clobbered on U.S. 380 just outside of the Lincoln cutoff from Route 70 (it had materialized, like a ghost, out of the hills that road winds through and I, with the family similarly aghast, had been unable to avoid it); the dog that had drowned in the pond of the state park in Capitan, home of Smokey the Bear, a mongrel that would not be revived no matter how much I pounded its chest or breathed into its maw; the red thing, big as a Shetland pony, that dragged Pam through a hedge and needed to be on property sizable as New Hampshire; our best friends' dogs, Sadie, Lilly, and Bootsie: the Larry, Curly, and Moe of the canine kingdom. No, with Al, all those others vanished from memory. This time, I vowed, it—I, me, us together—would be different. Better.

And for a time—more drama from a storybook—it was. She grew, learned to lie-down-sit-roll-over-play-dead-say-I-love-you-shake-hands as one complicated and joyful move. She played Frisbee, shagged golf balls, played split end on the family football team, and told us when the mail carrier put the bills in our box. She learned "no," a word not much used then or now, and "stay," and three or four others the experts tell us it's in the best interest of pets to recognize. Best of all, she learned to like everybody, especially folks you meet from the front seat of a car. Which meant—surely you're a step ahead of me now—a "day" had to cometh.

Specifically, she ran away. To High Street, one of our suburb's busiest, at rush hour. Across the field our street dead-ends at. Through the lot of the real-estate firm. Across the bank lot. Way out of sight. We didn't know, of course. Pam and Kelly and I were out looking. Up the block. Around the corner. She was over a year old and, we thought, well trained. We asked our neighbors—Flippo, Millie, even the grouch at the corner. *Nada.* Onto another street we charged. We described her: black and white, up to the knees, fast as Superdog, hair like a seal's, might smooch you to death. Nope, everyone said. Sorry. So very, very sorry.

Twenty minutes later, like insight to a fanatic, the obvious occurred to me. So off I went, at a pretty good clip myself. Past the realty office. Past the bank. All the way to High Street, traffic thick as mosquitoes in Canada. A Worthington cop was directing traffic. A wild man, I hailed him. He, bless his heart, put two and two together, came up with the Wonder

Dog. I'd just missed her, he said. She'd made herself another friend. I was relieved. But concerned. Where was she? Ah, he said, another police officer had her in the back of a patrol car. If I hustled, we'd catch them at the animal shelter.

Sure enough. There she was. In the back of a black-and-white. A fugitive. Tail going like a buggy whip, making pals with one of Worthington's gun-toting finest. Which led to a reunion. And a promise to put her collar, with tags, back on. We thanked everybody, authorities near and far. Maybe a prayer or two went up as well. Al, happy days, was home again. Later that evening, we had a discussion, Al and I. We were sitting on the deck (well, it's more like a porch without railings, not big enough to even cook out on, much less to throw a bash upon). She seemed contrite, thoroughly shamed, her eyes doing that thing only a dog's eyes can do. I wasn't afraid of her, I said. Just for her. She had to promise, cross her heart, never to do that again. For a second, she seemed to ruminate upon the matter. She hadn't been hungry, I knew. Nor was there anything romantic nearabouts to sniff.

It's hard watching a dog make up its mind. So I waited. The sun was down, darkness falling fast and heavy, another day in the book God keeps. Across the lots, lights were going on for dinner or TV news. More discussion seemed in order, so I commenced talking to her, not too odd a thing to do in a world reported to be full of angels and cult murderers and posses hiding out in cellars in Utah. I told her about how it was, lovewise, between me and her kind. I told her the Chockie story, the Phideaux story, and all the sad stories in between. I said she could go on sleeping at the foot of our bed, that we'd never chain her to a tree outside, that I'd never spank her. She'd get Alpo, I said. Whatever her heart desired. Tomorrow we'd go to Pet Paradise. Buy a pile of toys, chew sticks, her very own Nerfball.

That's what did it, I think. The Nerfball.

Okay, she said, in command of colloquially correct dog-talk.

You sure? I asked, not the only dumb question humans ask.

She was. So we went indoors—Al to the couch, me eventually to the typewriter. I had news for my former teacher. Specifically, I had to tell him about all the other questions dogs ask of the world they inhabit. What's in the bag? for example. Is it time for our walk yet? Did you hear that noise, stupid? Why so stingy with the wet food, fella? And so on. Questions every day—indeed, every hour—all of them important as any we ask of ourselves. Questions you dare not answer incorrectly lest you find yourself wandering the neighborhood, leash in hand, calling out the name of the only sentient creature in the universe that wants nothing from you but a scratch behind the ear.

HALF-MOON
Sheila Metzner

My family has owned two Bernese mountain dogs. Buddha, the puppy, is the second, and he belongs to my thirteen-year-old son, Louie. They are at the beginning of a long friendship. My first son, Raven, also had a Bernese mountain dog when he was thirteen, and since Mo, our family's first dog, has passed on, I asked Raven to evoke a moment in their relationship as a tribute of sorts to a noble and faithful friend. —SHEILA METZNER

Sunday afternoon, when it was time to leave my family's country house and my father was putting the bags in the car, we kids would go out on the front porch to find the dog. We would stand on the cold stone and yell for Mo. We would walk onto the lawn, my sisters and I, and shout. In the summer, the grass would be long and full of dandelions, and Stella would run to the backyard barefoot and look for him near the pumpkins and tomatoes, or by the peonies, where he loved to dig. Ruby and I would stand and wait for a few minutes and then yell again. Bega would walk the path to the riverbank, cupping her hands around her mouth and screaming for Mo until we could all hear the echoes over the water. Then we would sit on the porch and wait.

In the winter, when the grass was matted under the snow and the trees reached like skeletal hands into the gray sky, we would hear Mo coming from a distance. The sound of brittle branches snapping and brambles parting would let us know he was closer. Stella would spot him on the bridge, or Louie would hear his thunderous footsteps coming up from the riverbank. Suddenly, out of nowhere, from around a bend of fence or from behind the gristmill or from under a low bush, he would appear—Mo, his wide shoulders rolling with exertion and his tongue wagging out of his mouth in a flurry of warm breath as he lumbered toward us. His great black coat would be wet or covered with briars, his white-socked feet coated with river mud or black dirt from the clover fields. He would come and Ruby would grab him and hug him, because he was big enough to be hugged, big as a bear. She would pull the brambles from behind his ears while my parents drank their after-dinner coffee in the kitchen. He would sit on the porch then with us, legs spread behind him, face raised and noble. He looked like an illustration, a stylized woodcut of a dog, a statue of a dog.

Since Mo is gone now, my parents, sisters, and brother and I have discussed his moments alone in the wilderness. We have smiled together while watching our new Bernese

Sheila Metzner

puppy, Buddha, barking and scampering in the front yard. We sit and remember our proud monster Mo, with his sad blue eyes and white-tipped tail, wandering in the marsh or the pine forest, sniffing through the briars and exploring the woods, his territory. He must have heard our voices from wherever he was—the edge of a stream, the center of a cornfield, the tip of a cow pasture. He would hear our call and come home at a run. He would crash through the night across the snow and return to us.

Asleep on the ride home I used to dream that the distances he traveled were immense. In my night imagination, Mo could have been exploring the Gobi desert or trekking across alpine ridges. He might have chased antelopes across the Serengeti or held at bay a pack of wild wolves on a rock-strewn ridge. I saw him like that in my dreams, midleap, his great paws held high and his tail straight behind. But when he heard our distant, muffled voices he would pause and turn on the spot to run back to us. He would crash through the bushes, the oases, the reeds and mud flats and return to us. Mo was the kind of dog that knew how to travel that sort of distance. Mo was short for Half-Moon, and in that moment when he stopped and heard our voices, his wet breath warming the dusk's night air, he could have been as far away as any constellation. —RAVEN METZNER

SHEILA METZNER

128

SHEILA METZNER

The Kiss Patrol

Armistead Maupin

Some dogs, I'm told, like to stick around when their owners are making love. They'll sit stone still and watch the proceedings with deadpan intensity, as if collecting evidence for some evil congressional subcommittee. Not Willie. As soon as human passion rears its ugly head—and he has an uncanny eye for the precise moment—he flings himself off the bed and skulks away to another room. This is jealousy, I suppose, mingled with mortification, though I'd like to believe there's an element of courtesy involved as well. In any event, he comes rocketing back only seconds after the deed is done, reclaiming his rightful place between us with breathless little yelps of relief and celebration. You'd think we'd just returned from a month in Europe.

Kissing is another matter entirely. If Willie finds us smooching in the kitchen before dinner, he'll proceed to bark indignantly until we've stopped. "Break it up, you jerks," he seems to be saying. "There are three of us here, remember?" I'm sure the late Mrs. Woodhouse would have found something deeply disturbing about this behavior, but Terry

and I are rather charmed by it. We've even named it, I'm loathe to admit—the Kiss Patrol—and have come to accept these yapping sessions as the poodle's only viable way of asserting his place in the family.

Yes, he's a poodle. We don't broadcast that fact widely, since there are all those lingering stereotypes about homos and their FiFi-dogs. Willie's not a FiFi-dog; he's butch in the way that short men sometimes are, tight as a bedspring and buoyantly scrappy. His color is officially red, the rich brick red of an Irish setter, and since we've never abused him with a topiary haircut, most people see him as a sort of animated teddy bear, a living Steiff creature. He's quite a manly little dog, really.

*

Willie and I have been together two years longer than Terry and I have. I bought him twelve years ago from a man who had a serious fixation on Steinbeck's *Travels with Charley*. Poor Willie—who's a miniature, not a sturdy standard like Charley—had spent the first six months of his life touring America in the back of a van, an experience that left him with a lifelong distaste for vehicular travel. His previous owner had called him K-Y, a lame joke I might have retained for the sake of continuity had I not all too vividly pictured myself in Dolores Park yelling out the name of the popular lubricant. So I rechristened him Willie, in part because I liked the simplicity of it, in part because the Princess of Wales had recently given birth to a son named William.

The new moniker was fine by him though, of course, we never fully obliterated the old one. For a while I would meet strangers on the street, people from Willie's Steinbeckian past, who would recognize that auburn coat and blurt out his maiden name, and he'd be all over them like a cheap suit. Sometimes even today, just for drill, Terry will utter a soft "K-Y" while Willie lies snoozing on the sofa, and Willie will look up and hoist his ears in befuddled recognition, like an old man hearing the nickname his buddies used to call him in the army.

As fate would have it, I met Terry on Willie's third birthday, though I didn't take note of this oddity until a year or so later, when I was studying the dog's family tree. Now October 16 is a big deal at our house, the only high holy day we still observe with any degree of regularity—our mutual anniversary/birthday. I know this is way too cute for most people to handle, but what the hell. When the universe sends you such a blazingly obvious sign, such a cornball bolt out of the blue, there's not much you can do but acknowledge it.

When Terry moved from Atlanta into my three-room cottage above the Castro, the dog was as thrilled about it as I was. After all, this new guy brought him treats and rubbed the insides of his ears and engaged him in long, intimate conversations. And Willie showed his gratitude by learning a stunning array of new tricks: how to circle the block off the leash, how to sit, how to wait dutifully at the curb until Terry gave the signal to cross the street. It was a new era suddenly, rife with possibilities. A certain easy symmetry had come to our household, and Willie knew it.

We've moved twice since then, first to a walk-up penthouse in the Mission District, where Willie entered middle-age and began to write his memoirs on the upholstery. Then, last year, Terry and I bought a house on the edge of Sutro Forest, thereby adding dirt and shrubbery to Willie's growing roster of urinary pleasures. He's become grumpier with age, I'm afraid. The little Pit Poodle can't walk to the mailbox without attempting, however unsuccessfully, to terrorize the neighbors. At home, though his ursine charm remains intact, he's grown ever more demanding, never satisfied with a two-handed backrub when a four-handed one is possible.

Who knows what's behind all this need? I suspect he never fully recovered from a time in the early nineties when Terry and I spent our winters away from him. On a larky impulse at the end of a long book tour we'd bought a farmhouse on the South Island of New Zealand. Since Willie would never have endured the brutal six-month quarantine required by that country, we decided to leave him home with our friend Steve, who, in spite of serious concerns of his own, had sweetly agreed to house-sit.

Willie adored Steve and enjoyed his company immensely, but the dog pined for us nightly, Steve said, waiting solemnly at the top of the stairs for our imminent return. We were gone five months the first year, three the second, building our nest on a golden slope above the South Pacific. And though we strung a rope hammock and planted a lemon tree and left saucers of milk for the hedgehogs, the place never seemed completely ours without Willie there.

A portrait of our absent companion, sent to us by our artist friend Darryl, became the chief icon of our Kiwi house. In the style of a hokey fifties postcard, its message read: Greetings from Willie, Poodle of Enchantment.

So maybe Willie has a right to be nervous. He knows how much it hurts to be left behind and doesn't plan on letting it happen again. Though we sold the place in New Zealand almost two years ago, Willie still keeps a wary eye on the hall closet, where the dreaded black nylon luggage is stored. And when Terry heads off on his frequent daylong rounds of shops and doctors and drugstores, and doesn't return by nightfall, the dog will sit anxiously by the door, inventing scenarios.

At times like those, I wish we had a common language. I would tell Willie not to worry, that Terry will be home any minute now, no worse for wear, that the evening will still be ours to share. But I would also have to tell him, as best I could, about the dark constancy that has shaped our lives for the decade the three of us have been together. I would explain why Steve never comes to visit anymore and why, in spite all the good things we both feel about Terry, we might not always have him with us in the bed.

Greetings from WILLIE
POODLE OF ENCHANTMENT

DARRYL VANCE

Bear, Bull, Bubba, and Other Folk

Robert Canzoneri

Bear, our first Old English sheepdog, wasn't our dog. Despite his superiority in hearing, smelling, and growing hair, he was one of us people.

He made it clear as a pup, when he became an invalid at the same time Candy did, that he knew what his position was. Bear had a slightly burned paw from stepping on a cigarette; as to Candy's ailment, I remember only that it was not, as it had been with Thurber's uncle, whatever was killing the chestnut trees that year. In any case, she took to bed, Bear establishing himself on the floor beside her, and I became doctor, nurse, and orderly.

Every time I gave Candy a drink of water I'd hear a little yippy bark. "Oh," I'd say. "You need water too?" He'd lie there regal as the Sphinx until I brought his bowl from the kitchen and put it between his front paws.

Next time, the yip would be for an ice cube, or a puppy treat. Finally, after a couple of days, I felt that I'd been through one yip too many.

"There's nothing wrong with you, now," I told him. "You know where your water is."

Bear looked up at me for a moment, sighed, hauled himself to his feet, and walked without the slightest limp to the kitchen.

Some folks, and I am often among them, like dogs better than people; Bear's preference was the other way around, with the exception of his one case of puppy love. He and Nadine made an odd pair at play: he a furry black-and-white bumblebee; she a small beaglish blur, banking turns along the backs of couches and halfway up the walls.

When he'd hear her at the front door, he'd rush to the light cotton blanket he slept on, drag it to his food bowl, and swirl it with his nose into a cover shaped like a beehive hairdo. Every few minutes he'd detour from their frantic romp, nose the blanket open, check inside, nudge it closed again, and run back to cut Nadine off and nip at her haunches.

He treated humans differently. He didn't nip at their haunches, although he might have if they'd gone about on all fours. When they rang the doorbell, he went not to hide his food but to the door; when it opened, he went through it.

There is, according to a book on the breed, no way to train Old English sheepdogs not to jump up on people; Bear never tempted us to quibble with that assertion. On into his 100-pound adulthood, even with us yanking and holding down and pulling at his collar when grown people came to visit, he managed to rear up and greet them nose to nose. His personal best was a both-paws-on-both-shoulders hello that put a six-foot, 200-pound man flat on his back on the porch and shook the house like a temblor.

Bear's interest in visitors abated not a whit after they made it into the house. As long as they were standing—the herding trait bred into his ancestors had not atrophied—he'd work whatever group there was into a tiny wad. When they got seated, if they'd let him or couldn't help it, he'd have his forepaws in their laps and their faces would be covered with kisses. If they managed to keep his feet on the floor, he'd drape his chin over a thigh. If they still didn't take to him, he'd go to the kitchen, we'd hear an ominous lapping sound, and he'd hurry back to try the routine all over again with his hairy chin a swamp.

Human babies fascinated him. He would rise up crib-side to check on my first grandson, but never so much as touch him with his nose. He was also good with my two-year-old granddaughter, a few years later, but as if they were siblings he coveted one of her toys. When naptime came, Niki would pile all her belongings near the back door. Bear would creep over when she was out of the room, rummage

through until he came up with her little squeaky pig, and take him off to his own private places. As soon as Niki woke, she would search through the house, find Piggy, and put him back where he belonged.

For days, Piggy went back and forth; fortunately, Niki's parents found its twin in a local toy store and left the original to belong to Bear forever. He took good care of his Piggy, grooming him mornings and taking him out into the yard from time to time to relieve himself. Once when we walked up to the office of a friend at the college, Bear surprised us by carefully setting Piggy on the floor for his share of the visit. He'd even tote Piggy, unseen within that hairy muzzle, for a two-mile walk, nuzzling him at the end as if to say, Wasn't that nice, now?

On his walks Bear made friends with people of all sorts. The littler ones responded to him instantly, as if he were a big furry stuffed toy. Bear would give a quick kiss to each face in the seething clumps of kids we walked through every schoolday morning; then he would move aside and sit, allowing them to crowd him with hugs and pettings, and with sweet nothings to whisper in his ear.

He learned when the mob of preschoolers at a day-care center had their recess, and suffered himself to be admired when they were let out of their fenced-in playground to wallow all over him. One day, even though the time and weather were right for the kids to be out, the playground was empty. Bear studied it a moment, and then pulled us to the door we'd once seen the kids go in and sat to wait.

How he knew the days they should be out and the days they shouldn't, we never learned. Nor did we discover how he knew when Sunday rolled around, but he did. He had always been very fond of Marge and Bob, who lived across the back fence. After Bob died, every Sunday when we got to the end of our cul-de-sac he took a right instead of the usual left and tugged us around the end of the block to see Marge. He would accept a good petting from her, then lie at her feet to absorb the conversation.

Travel broadened his range of human friends even further. In those days Candy played, and I played at, tennis, and since our travel agent assured us that dogs were specifically welcome, we tried a tennis-weekend package at a resort in the Alleghenies. Thus began Bear's reign at Bedford Springs Hotel.

Bedford Springs was a watering place dating back to nearly 1800 — a large, columned brick building nestled back against a mountain, with long balconied wooden sections added on like old riverboats rammed into each other. The staff were mostly local people, many of whom had worked there all their working lives. They took to Bear immediately.

The bellhops gave him treats; the cleaning women visited with him; the guests adored him. One elderly woman was so overcome when she spotted him down the corridor that she plopped down spraddle-legged on the carpet to hug him. He let her.

We would sit, evenings before dinner, in front of the fireplace in the huge lobby and have drinks; if we forgot to order ice cubes for Bear, Hazel, the barmaid, would scold us and bring him a bucketful anyway. Fresh ice cubes were fine, but those slightly used by people were even better. As a drink got low, he'd bend his will upon it until the last sip had been taken and the first ice cube was being crunched between his teeth.

Mr. Doyle, the maître d', would step out of the dining room at the top of the double staircase and bark at Bear before coming down to rub his ears. Guests would come in the front doors, head across the lobby toward the elevator or the ballroom, and suddenly veer in a group, like birds all turning together in the wind, to flock around Bear, who lay waiting to receive them, and give him what must have seemed all the attention in the world.

On our first trip to Bedford Springs, while Candy and Bear were trying not to watch me struggling through a tennis lesson, Bear lured a guest over who introduced herself as having had, and of course loved, an Old English sheepdog. Bear took to her so specially that at dinner that evening, Candy nodded toward her and her husband at a nearby table and whispered to me, "She's Monica and his name is Leslie. Go ask him if he'd like to play tennis tomorrow."

"I luh?" I said. Having taught myself the game all wrong as a boy, and having not played for nearly a quarter-century, I was trying to relearn "correctly." My game was at the I'm-not-quite-sure stage that leaves the ball pretty much out of it.

"Ask him," she insisted, so, reluctantly, I did.

Turned out Leslie's game suited mine pretty well. We didn't play points but lobbed the ball back and forth at a leisurely pace, interrupted from time to time when Leslie would meander toward the net with some remark beginning, "As the bishop said to the actress. . . ."

All this gave Bear and Candy and Monica time to plot out our lives for a few years to come. We'd meet at Bedford Springs a couple of times a year, usually spring and fall. Misty early mornings Candy and I would follow Bear across to his paddling hole in the mountain stream, then along rocky trails through leafing or golden trees. Bear would have a rest in the room while we had breakfast, but afterward he would take Leslie and Monica and us for a second morning walk.

Often he had even a third walk with one of us and Monica—who had a back injury that kept her off the tennis court—along the creek through the golf course, watching whole families of groundhogs work in and out of their hole in a high bank, or spotting hawks or giant pileated woodpeckers.

After our lunch and an essential nap, Bear would take us on yet another long walk up mountain trails, with a detour to an open field where we'd pass the football for him. He'd run back and forth, often hitting the receiver with a body slam worthy of the NFL; when he got the ball he'd have us chase him, showing off his superior moves by keeping it just out of reach.

The days would be capped by preprandial drinks, with Bear in the receiving position, in front of a comfortable fire, then a great dinner, postprandial drinks with Bear again receiving, and a final walk through the moonlight or starry dark. One evening toward the end of the hotel's existence, Mr. Doyle put the five of us in a small dining room with a phalanx of waiters, waitresses, barmaids, and barmen—by then all Friends of Bear—and served up a big bowl of chocolate ice cream for Bear.

The Bedford Springs visits didn't give Leslie and Monica as much Bear as they wanted, apparently; soon they invited him, and Candy and me, to their home. Their main living area, featuring Monica's baby grand piano, was separated by glass walls from Leslie's rose garden, a strip of pheasant-haunted woods, and a patio with a friendly resident chipmunk.

When Monica played Mozart for us, the chipmunk and a rabbit and several birds would form a half-circle outside the big windows to listen, as if animated by Disney. Wherever he was lying, Bear would look up as the Mozart began, then rouse himself and sit beside her through the entire piece with one paw set gently on the piano just above the treble keys.

Because of Monica's back problem, we worried about Bear's tendency to jump up on people. He had a stubborn tendency, also, to ignore our commands unless he'd had reasons spelled out for him in detail. Why he must never jump up on Monica was a far more remote and abstract concept than why he should come inside or not chew a ball into pieces, but before our first visit we tried explaining anyway.

He behaved beautifully until one night at dinner when Monica said, "Oh, Bear, I forgot to bring your apple," and went through the swinging door to the kitchen. Bear loved apples; he sat bending his will upon the door, waiting. As she came back through, he rose up to full height, his paws headed for her shoulders. Monica froze, apple slice in hand, and so did we all. Including Bear. He lowered himself carefully to the floor without touching her, slunk over beside my chair, lay down, and covered his eyes with his paws.

The fact that he loved Monica was not remarkable; everybody did. But that was hardly the case with Bull. Bull wasn't the man's real name, of course; but, then, Bear wasn't Bear's—he was christened Mr. Micawber, which gradually reduced through Micawber to Caw-Bear to Bear. Early on, Candy gave him yet another nickname, which stuck with some of his fans and just may have had something to do with his friendship with Bull.

Candy and young Mr. Micawber were in the vet's waiting room with several lean, weather-beaten men in grimy overalls, each with a brace of hounds. After a few minutes, one of the men cut his eyes toward the furry little nonhound and demanded, "Whut's 'at dog's name?" Candy was sure that if she said, "Mr. Micawber," every hound in the place would be turned loose on him, so she blurted out, "Bubba."

Bubba, or Bear, got to know Bull through our everyday walks, which took us through the cemetery, along tree-lined streets, up to the college, sometimes around uptown Westerville, and occasionally to the library. Bear got to be friends, and saw to it that we did too, with people who lived along his routes, as well as the sexton and workers at the cemetery, the city's garbage handlers, and all the street crews.

The brick streets of Old Westerville have to be torn up sometimes to get at water mains or whatever. Bull was the expert at relaying the paving bricks, which he handled as if they weighed no more than dominoes. He had thick arms and the sort of beer belly that must get its name from being shaped like, and as hard as, an old-fashioned beer keg. Records Bull had established as a fast-pitch softball player still stood after many years. We were told that when he got mad at a batter, he'd simply break his arm with a fastball. His helpers, it was obvious, were a bit afraid of him.

At first we would just happen upon Bull; Bear would waggle up to him as he would to anybody, and Bull would give him a gruff, "Hi, boy," petting him with as rough a hand as ever existed. But the relationship grew.

Through much of Bear's life his object on setting out in the morning was to find Bull—and he could do it. Some days we'd wonder why he was tugging us through streets we seldom walked, when far up ahead we'd see barriers and a city truck, then Bull's thick body bent to the street bed.

As time went on the scene of their meeting became panoramic. One of Bull's helpers would spot us at a distance and say, "There he comes"; we could tell because Bull would straighten up as if startled, hurry to the truck, get out his jacket, and grapple in a pocket for a dog biscuit.

By then Bear would be pulling like crazy. If the streets were clear of traffic, we'd let go of his leash, and he and Bull would run to each other like long-separated lovers on a heathery hillside in some romantic movie. In retrospect I see them in slow motion and can hear background music coming to a crescendo as credits begin to roll against a fade-out showing a sort of heavenly future.

Marge's Bob had gone first. Bull outlived Bear— who didn't quite make it around to Marge's one Sunday morning—just long enough to meet "Little Bear," his successor and near look-alike. Bull's "Little Bear," really named Topper, outlived Niki. All of them are there in the fade-out—an unlikely grouping, perhaps, but herded quite happily together by Bear, probably with Piggy, who disappeared years ago, held ready to be placed carefully among them.

STANLEY AND BOODGIE
David Hockney

Stanley and Boodgie sleep with me, so we know each other
very well. I know all their little ways, lying with their legs in
the air and so on. My pictures of them are very tender. I had
to put drawing boards all around the house and studio, and
pick up the paper quickly wherever they were.

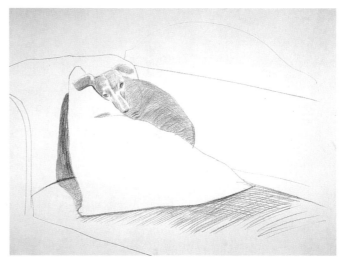

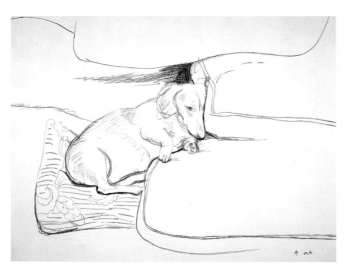

DAVID HOCKNEY

Lassie Come Home: Smart Design's Dog House
Tucker Viemeister

In 1989 Cooper-Hewitt, the Smithsonian Institution's National Design Museum, in New York, asked some designers to propose doghouse designs for a summer garden exhibition co-sponsored by Guiding Eyes for the Blind. The curators thought the subject of doghouses would interest many audiences, including blind people, since many of them have Seeing Eye dogs (even though Seeing Eye dogs live inside their master's house).

In summer 1990, twenty-four doghouses were displayed in the backyard of the Carnegie mansion, which houses the Cooper-Hewitt. The exhibit was a big success, attracting many blind people and their guide dogs, as well as lots of sighted people and, only for this exhibit, some hot dogs.

At Smart Design, where I'm a founding member, we always begin our design process by considering how we can use the project to make a positive contribution to our culture. We look at the context of the object and the needs of the people are who going to use our design. Doghouses have two user groups: the dog and the owner. Throughout history humans have shown extraordinary concern for pets. But like other domesticated animals, dogs seem happy to live anywhere as long as they are with their master. A dog doesn't care if its home is new or how much it costs or what it looks like. Modern designers grappling with our postindustrial world crisis can learn a lesson from dogs' behavior. The intention of design is not mere products; we can no longer design for consumption. As Mies van der Rohe said, Less is more—both economically and environmentally.

For the Cooper-Hewitt doghouse project we considered three user groups: the dog, the owner, and the viewing public. All great product designs are more than perfectly functioning objects; they also strike a chord in us.

People need a mental handle to connect with a pan, just as much as they need a physical handle to pick it up. The psychonomic aspects of a doghouse designed for an exhibition are more important than the ergonomic factors. A beautiful chair seems more comfortable than an ugly one. The designers' audience today is looking for a good bone—an emotional connection—more than some shiny new stuff.

Garbage is not only a renewable resource; it was our inspiration. We did not want to make more "designer" junk. We wanted to turn junk back into useful artifacts. What epitomizes the great wasteland more than a junked television set—the discarded shell of our technology?

The premier conduit of popular culture is television. It has become man's electronic best friend—loyal, dependable, lovable, and entertaining. The superstar dogs—Lassie, Rin Tin Tin, Pluto, Astro, and Benji—live there; Snoopy's been there. The distinction between technology and pets will continue to blur as we move into the next millennium.

From a purely practical point of view, a discarded console makes a pretty good doghouse. We modified a solid plastic console we found in a TV repair shop; adding a corrugated fiberglass roof to keep rain and snow from collecting on the flat top. A coat of blue Sears Weather

Beater paint transformed a piece of twentieth-century refuse into a trashy domicile complete with a built-in picture window and rabbit-ear antenna.

We call our creation Lassie Come Home because the literary play on words echoed our design's play on ideas. We all yearn for the comfort of those black-and-white years — but since we can't go back, we must do it better. We know that our injection-molded colonial-style TV will last longer than the postmodern or hand-crafted dog houses shown that summer. We realize that dogs have a much more critical sense of smell than of aesthetics. In fact, when the show opened, the dogs liked Michael McDonough's best — it was made completely from dog biscuits! But our doghouse was very popular with the press, especially TV. Is that another lesson for designers?

TUCKER VIEMEISTER

By Definition
Roger Caras

Looking back, I can't really pinpoint where it began, much less when or why or how. My love of dogs has been like a birth defect or, more properly, a gift. Perhaps, after all, it is genetic and there is no where or when. Anyway, it has always been there, this dog-love thing.

When I was born, in rural Massachusetts in 1928, there was already a mature dog in the family. His name was Bozo and he was an outsize Boston terrier. It seems as if everybody owned Boston terriers in those days, and a lot of them were large by today's standards.

Bozo was a pleasant enough dog, with a throaty bark I would later come to associate with pugs. I don't recall much about the end of Bozo, but I do remember it was a conscious decision by my parents. I was six or seven,

and I remember trying to understand the whole life-and-death equation. I cried a lot, but the answer to the equation escaped me.

Bozo was followed by a collie. He was with us for so short a time that I don't recall his name. I do remember him dying. He had gotten a chicken bone out of someone's rubbish, and we found him dead on our front lawn. I remember staring down at him and then kneeling. I reached out and touched him, but I still didn't understand.

Later there was an English cocker, named Peter, and he was a real companion. I was nine when we got him and my love affair with dogs blossomed. If I was not in school, Peter was glued to me like a limpet. From that day to this I have never been comfortable without a dog nearby. I feel incomplete. Fortunately my wife, Jill, feels the same way. We have eleven dogs at the moment. Over our forty years together or so, I would guess we have had fifty, and although we make vague noises about allowing natural attrition without addition to occur it just never happens. Some people (generally non-pet owners) believe that those of us who are "into" pets indulge ourselves in a kind of replacement activity. We are said to have failed in our human relationships or something like that. Well, who am I to argue with that kind of profound insight? I will just have to trudge along loving and being loved, accepting and not being judged, either. Things will probably never change.

In my study, where I come to write, lie three of my eleven dogs. Topi is a glorious golden whippet, Lizzie is a lovely basset bitch, and Duncan is a Border collie. Guy, a petite basset griffon Vendeen, is next door in a half-acre kennel run with Rose and Sweet William, our bloodhounds. Down at the main house, Sam the Yorkie lords it over the four rescued racing greyhounds, Lilly, Sirius (also spelled Xyerius), Dickens, and Reggie (or La Pomme de Terre du Lit, as he is also known). This is the first time in a long time that there haven't been some random-breds. Well, our

daughter who lives nearby has a lovely random-bred pooch among her five dogs. Oh, yes, I do believe it must be genetic. Our son's family is into cats. That could also be genetic. Jill and I have nine of them, too.

Why eleven dogs? Well, they make Jill and me feel comfortable. They round things out. (We have thirty-six pets in all.) When our grown kids come over with their kids (they practically live here) they often bring a dog or two or three. Rupert Rupert is a rescued chocolate Lab, Mollie is a Westie from the ASPCA shelter in New York City, and Chloe is a three-legged random-bred who was born with five legs. Two of them were useless, so off they came.

Is this excessive? Is it overdoing it to have a couple of thousand books on dogs and other pets here in my library (and thousands more on wildlife and ecology)? What about my collection of classic photographs of dogs and my collection of antique dog collars and, down at the house, Jill's superb collection of dogs in bronze and fine porcelain?

No, we are, with pride, down from the cavemen who were the first to know what dogs can be in people's lives. Dogs are not our whole life, but they make our lives whole.

BECAUSE OF LEELA
Tony Mendoza

I've never owned a dog. I'll blame this shortcoming on my vagrant history, my travel lust. But in my long career as a bachelor (I was married for the first time at forty-five), I've always had girl friends with dogs. I owe a huge debt to one such pet, Leela, who saved my artistic life in 1979. I had failed miserably at two professions, first as an engineer, then as an architect, and was rapidly but surely failing at my third attempt at a career, photography as art. I had been trying to make it as a photographer for four difficult years and was going nowhere fast. I was broke, dejected, ungranted,

Tony Mendoza

unknown, and unloved. Then I met Judy, Leela's mom, and quickly became enamored, first with Judy, then with Leela. The latter was so vivacious, funny, crazy, and photogenic that I started taking my first dog pictures. The pictures that resulted were weird, unlike any dog pictures I had ever seen before, so I took more pictures, and more. I became obsessed. Eventually Judy threw me out, since I was spending more time with her dog than with her, but the work endured. Armed with my dog pictures I moved to New York City, determined to give my art photography career one last shot. To my surprise, everyone loved my Leela pictures. A gallery gave me my first one-man, one-dog show, a well-known art magazine gave the show an excellent review, the Museum of Modern Art bought some prints, and last but not least, I won an NEA photography fellowship with the work. My art career was saved. All these successes gave me a lot of energy and confidence. More girls fell in love with me, and, of course, I kept taking pictures of their dogs. Finally, I met a wonderful woman. I fell head-over-heels in love and it was reciprocal. We married. She was a cat person. I became a cat photographer. Some years passed and we started renting a summer place in a small beach community in the Florida panhandle. It turned out that this beach was a favorite vacation spot for people with dogs. It didn't take long for me to start a new photographic project.

TONY MENDOZA

TONY MENDOZA

TONY MENDOZA

TONY MENDUZA

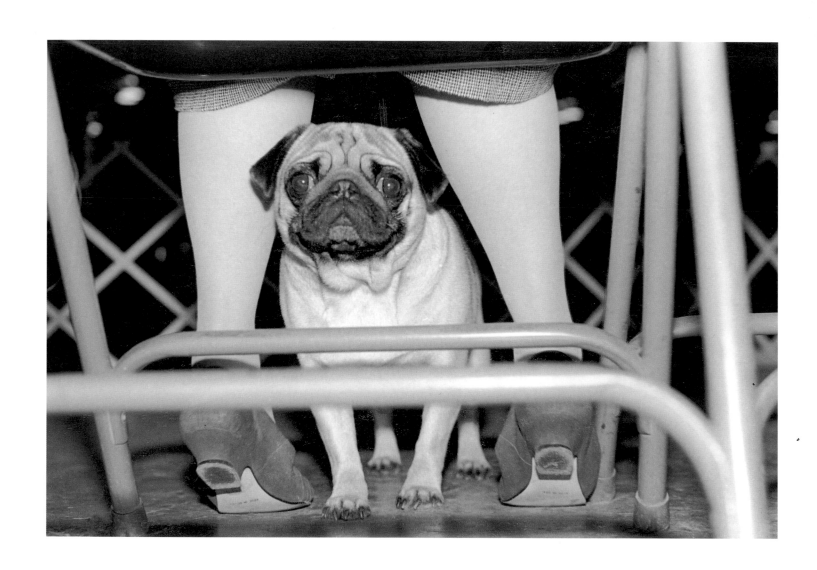

TONY MENDOZA

TONY MENDOZA

The Company of Canines

Bob Shacochis

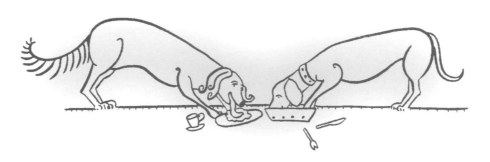

It is to republican Rome, a city and culture nourished by the milk of a wolf, that we trace our modern regard for dogs, even though in the fourth millennium B.C., the Chinese emperor Fo-Hi did consider breeding tiny dogs to slip into his robe as pocket warmers, and an ancient Egyptian would shave his head to mourn the death of his dog; and let's not forget that when Odysseus returned home after his twenty-year road trip, only Argus, his mutt, recognized him. Lucky Odysseus, to have a dog kept alive so long by loyalty. Indeed, the rise of civilization and the domestication of dogs were simultaneous events, both inspired by mealtimes around the campfire. Dogs and food, hunger and friendship, are bound together in the roots of prehistory. Our appetites, not the least for affection, produced the dog; he's our creation, made in our image, a household hanger-on.

So perhaps it's not in such good taste, so to speak, for me to whine as I do at Christmastime, when Miss F. bakes a month's worth of delicious cookies, though the first batch she makes are for the dog(s), *plural,* who seem to have eternally established a first-come, first-served agenda in our lives. I'm not sure I'm thoroughly pleased they've nosed themselves to the top of the list of priorities, but they in fact and deed have, morning, noon, and night, though for the past year, I have struggled to enforce a very few hard-and-fast rules around the house regarding matters canine, and the result, now evident, is that I've lost both the battle and the war.

Throughout our many years together, Miss F. and I have owned a dog, one, one moderately big dog, and as recently as six months ago, that one-dog role was nicely played by Issabel, a rather independent, willful, and self-amusing Irish setter who believes it's funny to ram her missile-like nose into your backside if you bend over to tie your shoes and who burps so loudly and insubordinately when you try to lecture her, you have to stop and wonder where she picked up all this rudeness—certainly not from me. Since Miss F. is now, thank God, employed and because I traveled too frequently this past year, Miss F. fretted that we had abandoned Issabel out on the brink of loneliness, left by herself in the house all day, not exactly starved for attention but increasingly under-nourished—and wouldn't it be kind and wise and fun to find her a companion? I didn't pause to think that this suggestion might be only a ploy of Miss F.'s in her lifelong campaign to surround herself with a court of dogs, she the loving queen of their affections, licked and panted over until the day she dies. She's never made it a secret that she expects to one day have at least five of them—a couple of setters, a standard poodle, a Jack Russell terrier, an Irish water spaniel—and I imagine there are a couple more breeds on her list that she's hesitant to tell me about. I think, though, that she thinks I'd appreciate being the alpha male of my very own pack.

Whenever she's gone on this way, I've always invoked Hard-and-Fast Rule Number One: You may have as many dogs as you wish, applying the formula of one dog per acre, and since our fiefdom in its most current survey extends to only about a quarter of that landmass, I have told her repeatedly that she's already exceeded her ceiling on dogs by a factor of four. Any waiver of the rule, I argued, would be madness.

Well, this reasoning seemed to have made quite an impression upon Miss F. She dropped the subject until this past October, at which time she was, not so coincidentally, admitted to the Bar; after that, I must say, it seemed that court was always in session around the palace as we sought to refine and tune the domestic code, which comes under a singular range of pressures with any addition to the fold. Miss F. advocated compassion and generosity for the latch-keyed Issabel. Since I am the unshaven and ill-dressed member of the family, you might assume I would therefore represent the libertarian, populist, underdog side of this issue, and Miss F., having thrown in her lot with the Established Order, would espouse the conservation of sanity and reason in our own self-made universe, but the bare truth is we have a set, however limited, of hard-and-fast rules around here because I want them, hoping to preserve some illusion of rationality in the days of our lives.

Right. Well and good. By November, the verdict was in the door, and his name was Frankie. I can't even recall the moment I acquiesced to this, though I'd like to believe Miss F. is not one of those monarchs who go in for drugging and backhandedness. Frankie was a handsome nine-month-old male with dancer's legs and foppish ears, a bit developmentally slow, who was able to communicate to us that, were he in fact human, his identity would be not unlike that of a baffled poet, who disdained physical love for spiritual knowledge and whose interest in the opposite sex was not merely platonic but noble to the point of canonization. Which we took to be the absolute truth because Issabel, a three-year-old tart, was in the middle of her semiannual estrus when Frank showed up, took one fastidious sniff of her, and asked for a copy of *The Complete Works of Robert Browning*. The threat of being bombed with puppies seemed deferred for another six months, at which time we could either expand the boundaries of the kingdom or have Issabel spayed. Meanwhile, as long as her heat continued, Issabel was allowed to receive only eunuchs and, of course, the asexual youngster Frankie.

Around the same time, I left town for a week, off to Miami to determine the gastronomic impact of the Noriega trial on the American judicial system (*arroz con pollo* has definitely infiltrated the U.S. attorney's office, though a Justice Department spokesperson vehemently denies this). While I was there, I got a frantic phone call from Miss F., who was in Cedar Key visiting friends and fellow dog owners. While Miss F. sat for tea with Miss Connie, the dogs were out back with their dog host, Hobbes, discussing the often subtle difference between leaves and birds. A brown Lab approached, perhaps with an insight about wind. Despite being neutered, he nevertheless became enamored with Issabel and pantomimed what he would do to her if only he were so equipped. Frankie, the retarded child-poet in a dog suit, feigned a distaste for such crude display, stepping aside to look on in a dim-witted but ponderous fashion. However, when Miss F. next glanced out the window, she saw what I have a great deal of trouble believing she had never seen before in her life, since she has seen most everything.

"Frankie and Issabel got stuck together!" she cried into the phone.

Today I have to honestly ask myself: "What the fuck were we thinking?" Spring is on its way as I write, and, by the mathematics of my Hard-and-Fast Number One, we are now operating at the ratio of forty dogs per acre, at the current net rate of being a ten-dog household, thanks to Issabel's litter of eight. Wouldn't it be easier if we just had a kid? I asked Miss F., and, maybe, well, yes, I finally got her to agree, so we're working on that with all the tenacity—speaking for myself—of Piers the Plowman, but that's another story. But I suspect Miss F. remains sympathetic to the views, conception-wise, of the African bushman who wondered why he should take up farming when there are so many mongongo nuts in the world. Or, as Cynthia Nelms has said, "I'd get pregnant if I could be assured I'd have puppies."

In the meantime, there are a few new hard-and-fast rules at our house—they are, of course, my rules, not Miss F.'s— and the majority of them apply to mealtimes. For instance: No dogs on the table during dinner. At the table is acceptable, to a point. No climbing up on guests, unless they are foolish enough to encourage it, or too inert or simply too stupid to knock the infractor away decisively, best accomplished by a rap with the flat side of a butter knife. Also, food that sits upon a guest's plate or is in transit from a guest's plate to a guest's mouth is, *ipso facto,* the guest's food and not doggy food, so lunging and running off with something is out, with this single exception: In the case of any ostentatious, long-winded, and tedious guest who, in the midst of fatuous monologue, continues to wave a sparerib or a chicken leg in the air like a baton and shake it aggressively at other members of the party while he or she advances such propositions as "The Japanese are predatorial little devils" or "We can save education in America without paying for it,"

the aforementioned sparerib or chicken leg may be torn unceremoniously from the speaker's hand and gulped down quickly, together with any fingers that come along as garnish.

I have also enacted an amendment to the above package of rules, to close a loophole wide enough for Frankie's tongue to have made its way through. Frankie is to tongue what Cyrano de Bergerac is to nose. The dog is perfectly capable of standing well back from the table, seemingly obedient, and, while mesmerizing you with the exquisite sensitivity and lugubrious soulfulness of his poet's eyes, curling his tongue out the side of his apparently closed mouth to discreetly bridge the distance between him and your table setting, laying this anatomical wonder down on a plate or into a bowl of soup with such surreptitious innocence that it's possible for you to think that he thinks that you think this enormous pink and pulsing slab of tongue nesting in your food is simply a part of the evening's culinary presentation, and no one need be alarmed. Once caught in this ruse, Frank seems quite satisfied to graciously reel his tongue back where it belongs with whatever trace of flavor or ribbon of sauce has adhered to its flypaper surface.

Frankie established his gastronomic agenda early on at our house by habitually eating the covers off Miss F.'s *Bon Appetit*s, yet he snubs the same high-quality brands of canned dog food that pensioners seem to enjoy so much at the end of the month. On the other hand, when he's in his ascetic poet mood, the big Frank adores the blandest kibble, holding each single comforting morsel in his mouth until it melts like a communion wafer delivered by the Pope. He's a queer one, Frank. In contrast, Issabel's aesthetic works off the theme of gluttony. She's been ravenous now for months, devouring, devouring, devouring, and begging constantly for treats, her two current favorites being hot pickled okra and Max's Italian Style Dog Snacks, all natural ingredients—as if she cares.

Back to the rules. There is no need to legislate the ownership of food that hits the floor, seeing as how there's been plenty of precedent since the dawn of time, that this food is fair game for man or beast.

Understand that I realize not everyone wants to eat in the company of dogs, though most of our closest friends do, or don't mind, or perhaps are afraid to speak out. From my own perspective, once they've let it be known that the dogs are OK, I imagine if anything's going to put them off, it's the sight of Miss F. using these poor creatures to circumvent the one household task she is explicitly sworn to, no matter what, even though this job is the one she is worst at in all the world: washing dishes. (Listen, I cook, don't bother me with that.) So Miss F. enlists the dogs to help with the dishes. I'm sure if she had her way entirely, they'd lick everything clean, far cleaner than she ever manages to get things in the sink, and all she'd have to do is stuff the plates right back into the cupboard. Our more regular guests already conspire in this routine and simply pitch their tableware onto the floor for a preliminary scrubbing once they've had their fill. I have yet to come up with a hard-and-fast rule that addresses any potential abuse or embarrassment that might develop from this, since Miss F. tells me that the mouths of Issabel and Frankie are cleaner than my own, and although I know this assertion is part of dog mythology, in my case I tend to believe her. (Miss F.'s only hard-and-fast rule, by the way, if you were wondering, is that anytime they so desire, the dogs may eat the mail.)

It's true that we've been occasionally blessed with a dinner guest so important and uniquely fascinating, such a paradigm of culture, such an example of genius and manners and hygienic vulnerability, that we've wrapped the dogs from head to tail in duct tape and thrown them out into the back- yard so as not to distract us from the utterance of the great man or great woman gracing our table. We'll do that for you, too, if you're that fucking wonderful and prissy. On the whole, though, Miss F. and I prefer our humanity rank and file, and for those of you on this earth, all of you nature respecters and admirers of things great and small, who find pets (or children) to be a vast annoyance, let me assure you that your invitation is not in the mail, and let me warn you that I have it from a pretty good source (the poet Frankie) that Saint Peter is actually a guard dog, a stern but nevertheless good-hearted Doberman pinscher, and he's going to want to know just what in the world it was you thought you were talking about, back on earth, when you talked about love.

RECIPE: COOKIES (DOG BISCUITS)
$1^1/_2$ cups unbleached flour
$^3/_4$ cup grated cheddar cheese
$^1/_2$ cup frozen peas and carrots, thawed
4 tbsp. butter
1 clove garlic, minced
milk

First, you should know that Miss F. doubles the amount of the above ingredients, not only because we have two huge dogs, but because these dog cookies are so genuinely good she eats a couple of them herself. (I've yet to meet the dogs halfway on this one.) Also, you should go out and buy a bone-shaped cookie cutter (though I confess I have no idea where Miss F. got hold of hers).

Bring cheese and butter to room temperature. In a large mixing bowl, combine all ingredients, adding just enough milk to form a moist ball with the dough. Chill for 2 hours.

Roll onto flour-dusted surface, cut into bone shapes; bake at 375 degrees for 15 minutes, or until light brown. Makes 2 dozen.

LEE K. ABBOTT *is the author of five collections of stories, most recently* Living after Midnight. *He is the director of the MFA program in creative writing at The Ohio State University.*

EDWARD ALBEE, *three-time Pulitzer Prize—winning playwright for* A Delicate Balance, Seascape, *and, most recently,* Three Tall Woman, *is probably best known for his perennially performed play* Who's Afraid of Virginia Woolf?. *Albee lives in New York and Texas.*

JAMES BALOG'S *books include* Anima, Survivors: A New Vision of Endangered Wildlife, *and* Wildlife Requiem. *His photographs are exhibited at prominent museums and galleries in North America and Europe and appear regularly in the world's leading magazines. A resident of Colorado, Balog is committed to the examination of humanity's relationship with the natural environment.*

KAREN BARBOUR *is the author and illustrator of* Mr. Bowtie, Nancy, *and* Little Neno's Pizzeria. *She illustrated* Flamboyan, Street Music, *and* Princess Scargo and the Birthday Pumpkin, *a Rabbit Ears video. Her illustrations appear regularly on book covers and in periodicals such as* The New York Times, Newsweek, Rolling Stone, Harper's, Vogue, Atlantic Monthly, *and* The Boston Globe. *Barbour lives in Inverness, California.*

STEVEN BAUER *has recently finished a novel entitled* The Seven Months of Winter. *The author of* Satyrday *as well as a collection of poetry,* Daylight Savings, *he directs the creative writing program at Miami University in Oxford, Ohio.*

ANN BEATTIE *is the author of several award-winning and critically acclaimed novels and story collections, including* Where You'll Find Me, Picturing Will, Love Always, Chilly Scenes of Winter, *and* Another You. *She lives in Charlottesville, Virginia, with her husband, Lincoln Perry.*

Among **FREDERICK BUSCH'S** *books are* The Mutual Friend, Harry and Catherine, *and* Closing Arguments. *His most recent is* The Children in the Woods: New and Selected Stories. *He is Fairchild Professor of Literature at Colgate University.*

AMY *and* **DAVID BUTLER** *own and operate Art of the Midwest Studio in Mt. Vernon, Ohio, where they create fine art, illustration, and design. They have exhibited their work widely and have clients nationwide.*

ROBERT CANZONERI, *author of fiction, poetry, and nonfiction books, explores the Westerville, Ohio, Alum Creek bottoms every morning with his wife, Candy, and their Old English sheepdog, Boots. They count among their dog friends Larry, Alex, Billy, Paris, Madison, Tootsie, Rudy, Max, Rosie, Mackie, Nikki, Bandit, Duke, Sammy, Ozzie, Scout, Katie, and Rusty.*

ROGER CARAS, *president of ASPCA, the oldest humane organization in the Western Hemisphere, is the author of more than fifty books on the subject of pets and wildlife, including* A Dog Is Listening *and* A Celebration of Dogs. *"The voice of the Westminster Kennel Club," he is a frequent guest on radio and television programs throughout North America.*

RON CARLSON, *a native of Utah, is a professor of English at Arizona State University. He is the author of four books of fiction, most recently* Plan B for the Middle Class.

SUSAN CONANT'S *Dog Lovers' Mysteries, featuring sleuth and canine-maven Holly Winter, include* Ruffly Speaking, Bloodlines, *and* Gone to the Dogs. *The 1991 and 1992 recipient of the Dog Writer's Association of America's Maxwell Award for Fiction Writing, she lives in Massachusetts with her husband and two Alaskan malamutes. Conant commits much of her time to rescue work and acts as state coordinator of the Alaskan Malamute Protection League.*

NANCY FRIDAY *lives in Key West, Florida, and Connecticut. The author of* My Mother/My Self, Jealousy, *and* Women on Top, *she is currently working on a book about feminism and beauty.*

TIMOTHY GREENFIELD-SANDERS'S *portraits are in the collections of the Museum of Modern Art, the Metropolitan Museum of Art, the Whitney Museum, and the National Portrait Gallery, among others. He has exhibited in New York at the Leo Castelli Gallery and the Mary Boone Gallery; his most recent exhibition of artist portraits was a retrospective at the Modern Art Museum of Fort Worth. His fashion and celebrity images can be seen regularly in* Harper's Bazaar, Vogue, L'Uomo Vogue, *and* The New York Times Magazine.

BRIAN HAGIWARA *is a photographer, painter, and industrial designer living in New York City. He works in still-life photography for numerous editorial and advertising clients, but his favorite subject and muse is his bulldog, Bunny.*

CYNTHIA HEIMEL *has written columns for* Playboy, The Village Voice, *and* Vogue. *Her books include* If You Leave Me, Can I Come, Too?; Get Your Tongue Out of My Mouth, I'm Kissing You Goodbye!; Sex Tips for Girls; Enough About You; *and* If You Can't Live Without Me, Why Aren't You Dead Yet? *She lives in New York City and Los Angeles.*

DAVID HOCKNEY —*photographer, designer, painter, illustrator—has exhibited his work internationally for the last twenty years.* David Hockney: A Retrospective *was published in 1988. He has been doing portrait and dog drawings since 1993.*

BEAUREGARD HOUSTON-MONTGOMERY *is a typical Manhattan housewife who occasionally writes articles for magazines from* Family Circle *to* Bound and Gagged.

FRANZ LIDZ *is a senior writer at* Sports Illustrated. *His 1991 memoir,* Unsung Heroes: My Improbable Life with Four Impossible Uncles, *was recently released as a film, with Diane Keaton directing. He lives 600 yards north of the Mason-Dixon Line with his wife, Maggie, daughters Gogo and Daisy, and llamas Edgar, Ogar, and Vanessa Snakehips.*

DEIRDRE MCNAMER, *author of* Rima in the Weeds *and* Sweet Quarrel, *has worked as a reporter for several western newspapers and the Associated Press, and periodically contributes short pieces to* The New Yorker. *She lives in Missoula, Montana.*

MERRILL MARKOE *is the author of* What the Dogs Have Taught Me *and* How to Be Hap Hap Happy Like Me. *She is also a monthly columnist for* New Woman *magazine.*

ARMISTEAD MAUPIN *is the author of seven novels, the most recent of which is* Maybe the Moon. *A six-hour adaptation of his first novel,* Tales of the City, *became the highest-rated drama series ever broadcast on PBS. He lives in San Francisco with his lover and partner, Terry Anderson.*

TONY MENDOZA is the author of two books about a cat, Ernie and Ernie's Postcard Book. He is also the author of Stories, a pictures-and-text autobiography. The recipient of numerous grants and awards for his photography, including three NEA fellowships and a Guggenheim, he has also received two creative writing fellowships from the Ohio Arts Council.

CHRISTINE HERMAN MERRILL developed a passion for animals as well as art at a very young age, painting her first portrait of a dog in 1968. A fourth-generation artist, Merrill has completed numerous commissions from around the country and Europe since 1975. She recently illustrated her first picture book, Animal Heroes, by George Ella Lyons.

SHEILA METZNER, a contemporary master in the worlds of fashion, portraiture, still life, and landscape photography, has distinguished herself for the past twenty-two years with her fine-art photographs, editorial and advertising assignments, exhibitions, and books. Metzner's images have been shown in galleries and museums throughout the world and are beautifully featured in two monographs, Color and Object of Desire.

STAN OLSON likes to paint, tell stories, and stand out in the prairie and smoke cigars. For sixteen years he has illustrated for magazines and two Rabbit Ear Production video/books, Johnny Appleseed and the forthcoming Parables.

ROBERT ANDREW PARKER'S etchings, watercolors, and paintings are featured in the permanent collections of museums including the Museum of Modern Art, the Whitney Museum, and the Metropolitan Museum of Art. He is also an accomplished children's book illustrator, whose dozens of award-winning books include Winter Journey, Randolph's Dream, and Pop Corn and Ma Goodness. He makes his home in Connecticut, where he contributes regularly to a wide range of magazines.

DANIEL PINKWATER is the co-author (with Jill Pinkwater) of Superpuppy: How to Choose, Raise and Train the Best Possible Dog for You. He is a regular commentator on National Public Radio's "All Things Considered." His recent novel, The Afterlife Diet, is published by Random House.

VLADIMIR RADUNSKY is the prize-winning artist of the maestro plays, The Pup Grew Up!; Hail to Mail; and Square, Triangle, Round, Skinny. He lives in Brooklyn with his wife and collaborator, Evgenia.

ROBERT ROSENBLUM is a professor of fine arts at New York University and has written widely on art from the eighteenth century to the present. Of these books and articles, his favorite is The Dog in Art from Rococo to Post-Modernism (1988). He lives in Manhattan, where his family joins him in the worship of an English bulldog named Archie.

STEVE RUSHIN is a senior writer for Sports Illustrated. People sometimes ask if it's true that he writes for Spots Illustrated, the canine literary journal. It is not true, Rushin replies regretfully.

BOB SHACOCHIS'S first collection of stories, Easy in the Islands, won the American Book Award in 1985. His second collection, The Next New World, was awarded the Prix de Rome from the American Academy of Arts and Letters in 1989. Swimming in the Volcano, his first novel, was a finalist for the 1993 National Book Award. A columnist for Gentlemen's Quarterly and a contributing editor for both Harper's and Outside magazines, Shacochis resides in Florida.

DANNY SHANAHAN has been a regular contributor to and cover artist for The New Yorker for more than fifteen years. His cartoons have been widely anthologized as well as collected in his own volumes, which include Lassie, Get Help! His first children's book, Buckledown the

Workhound, was published in 1994. Born in Brooklyn, New York, and reared with ten brothers and sisters in Connecticut, he makes his home in New Mexico.

For the last twenty years, WILL SHIVELY has created award-winning photographs for editorial, advertising, and commercial clients including Doubleday, Borden, Structure, Abercrombie & Fitch, Newsweek, and Dance Magazine. His first book for children, Fishing with Dad, illustrated with Polaroid dry-transfers, will be published by Artisan. Born in New York City, Shively currently works and resides in Columbus, Ohio.

ENID SHOMER'S stories and poems have appeared in The New Yorker, The Paris Review, and Poetry. She was the 1988 recipient of the Iowa Short Fiction Award and the John Simmons Short Fiction Award for Imaginary Men. Her books of poetry include Stalking the Florida Panther, This Close to the Earth, and the forthcoming Black Drum. Shomer lives in Florida.

JANE SMILEY is the author of eight works of fiction, including the Pulizer Prize—winner A Thousand Acres; The Age of Grief (nominated for a National Book Critics Award); and, most recently, Moo. She teaches at Iowa State University and lives in Ames, Iowa.

TUCKER L. VIEMEISTER is a founder of Smart Design Inc., a group of designers who create products, packaging, graphics, interiors, and strategies. Recent products include "Good Grips" universal kitchen tools, Corning's Serengeti sunglasses, Cuisinart's coffee makers, Black & Decker's Metropolitan toaster, and lots of other comfortable, practical, award-winning fun stuff. Viemeister lectures, juries, and teaches around the world. He recently edited the compendium Product Design 6.

WILLIAM WEGMAN has participated in more than one hundred solo and group exhibitions in the past twenty years. Most recently, his mellow Weimaraners were featured in an extensive traveling exhibit of his photographs for Cinderella and Little Red Riding Hood.

JAMIE WYETH once noted, "Everybody in my family paints—excluding possibly the dogs." As the third generation of a dynasty of American painters that includes his grandfather, N. C. Wyeth, and his father, Andrew Wyeth, Jamie is a sensitive observer of his rural surroundings—depicting livestock and other beasts with the same care and intensity he devotes to portraits of people.

DAN YACCARINO is an illustrator living in New York City. His work has appeared in children's books and publications around the world. Yaccarino has been a dog lover since his seventh Christmas, when he woke up to find his dog, Terry, giving birth to the last of her eleven puppies.

ARTHUR YURINKS, writer and director, is the co-founder of The Night Kitchen theater. His latest book is The Miami Giant. He lives in upstate New York and Nova Scotia.

CREDITS AND ACKNOWLEDGMENTS

The editor would like to thank Jennifer McNally for her invaluable assistance, as well as Lee K. Abbott, Elizabeth Arthur, Steven Bauer, Oliver Jones, and Peter Kross of The Company of Animals Fund. Likewise, grateful appreciation is extended to The Jefferson Center for Learning and the Arts, particularly Gloria Hunter and Donn Vickers.